University for the Creative Arts

Fort Pitt
Rochester
Kent   Tel: 01634 888734
ME1 1DZ   E-mail:
gatewayrochester@uca.ac.uk

Commander F. W. Lipscomb, OBE, RN
Illustrated by Malcolm McGregor

Historic Submarines

HUGH EVELYN LONDON

First published in 1970
by Hugh Evelyn Limited
9 Fitzroy Square, London W1
© 1970, Hugh Evelyn Limited
Designed by Lawrence Edwards
Printed in the Netherlands by
Joh. Enschedé en Zonen
SBN 238.78925.X

Contents

Colour Plates

Preface

To cover the evolution of the submarine within the limits of sixteen principal drawings and some 15,000 words of text demands concentration on those advances which have made outstanding contributions to the story. Fortunately, the submarine officers who have kindly given time and thought to the subject are agreed on the choices made for the illustrations and the principal points developed in the text.

So far as the drawings are concerned it must be understood that many submarines during their lifetime were considerably altered, particularly in respect of gun armament, and there are photographs and drawings of some of the submarines illustrated which do not correspond with the illustrations selected for this book.

During the writing of this book and while advising the artist on the 16 full-page drawings, the author has consulted numerous naval officers and civilians from many countries who have made detailed studies of the subject. Some of these have collected thousands of photographs, others have compiled whole libraries of books, articles and paper-cuttings, covering many aspects of design and capability. Nevertheless, in spite of this wealth of material, it is clear that there are still some features of design which have not been recorded and the precise origin of some important fittings cannot be exactly established. For example, it is generally agreed that Professor Marié Davy introduced the periscope in the French Navy in 1854, Drzewiecki and Goubet made primitive periscopes around 1879 and Captain Bacon designed his own for the British 'Holland' boats, but it is a matter of opinion as to who was the most significant innovator.

As regards hydroplanes, the French were again prominent in this development. Goubet and Gustave Zédé employed them in their drawings. Elsewhere Nordenfeldt and Holland made contributions and Waddington fitted hydroplanes to his submarine which he built in Liverpool in 1886.

Study of the schnorkel tube leads us to no firm conclusion as to its origin. Simon Lake fitted a tube to his *Argonaut* in 1895 and this may be considered to be the first example. Much later, in 1916, the well-known firm of Scott designed a fully operational tube. Nevertheless it was not until the Second World War that this fitting took its place as standard equipment, when the Germans appreciated its value in extending the endurance of their submarine fleet.

Turning to modern times, it must be understood that nuclear submarines are equipped with much classified material and information on such matters as sonar and radar has had to be omitted, from both the illustrations and the text.

Acknowledgements

In writing this book and assisting Malcolm McGregor to obtain sufficient and accurate material for his drawings, I have received generous help from many officers and civilian technicians. Unfortunately, space does not permit mention of all and I must ask the forbearance of those who are not named in person.

I am especially grateful to Admiral Sir Charles Little, G.C.B., G.B.E., one time Commanding Officer of *Holland IV*, for his invaluable help with the drawing of the 'Holland' type and for his experienced advice generally. Also Vice Admiral Sir Hugh Mackenzie, K.C.B., D.S.O., D.S.C., lately head of the British Nuclear Submarine Programme, who kindly checked the manuscript and gave most helpful advice, particularly on nuclear matters. As ever the Ministry of Defence (Navy) gave every assistance and I am grateful to Miss J. N. Price for her special interest. Mr Raymond V. B. Blackman, M.I.Mar.E., M.R.I.N.A., editor of *Jane's Fighting Ships*, Mr E. Clarke, Public Relations Officer, Vickers Armstrongs, and Lieutenant Commander G. H. F. Frere-Cork, R.N. (Retd.), Curator, Submarine Museum, H.M.S. *Dolphin*, have all made most valuable contributions and I owe them special thanks. Mr Osborn and Mr Tucker of the National Maritime Museum, and Mr J. Fulford, Director, and Mr R. Mayne of the Imperial War Museum, gave ready help at all times which was much appreciated. The help provided by Mr L. Honeywill of Newton Abbot, Devonshire, one time Chief Engineroom Artificer, who is an expert on historical detail, was extremely useful.

Abroad, my thanks go first to Monsieur Henri le Masson, Vice President of the Académie de Marine and editor of *Les Flottes de Combat*, who not only entrusted to me some irreplaceable documents but also sent me a copy of the manuscript of his own latest book *Du Nautilus au Redoutable*. Monsieur le Masson also read the manuscript of my book and made many most important suggestions and comments.

Members of the Staff of the Commander-in-Chief United States Naval Forces Europe could not have been more helpful and I am specially indebted to Captain S. H. Packer, U.S.N., and Commander H. E. Hetu, U.S.N. Mr Claud M. Ladd of the Office of the Assistant Secretary of Defence, Washington, D.C., sent most useful lists and comments. Mr S. J. Worman and Captain Frank Lynch, U.S.N. (Retd.), both of the General Dynamics, Electric Boat Division, Groton, Connecticut, did all in their power to answer the many questions put to them.

The Defence and Naval Attachés of Germany, Italy and Japan, resident in London, put me in touch with experts in their respective countries, notably Herr W. Grutzemacher of Diesenhofen.

Finally, I wish to record my warmest thanks to the publishers, particularly Mr Hugh Street, the Managing Director, for his understanding of the problems involved, and Miss Virginia Sherwin for much typing and retyping.

F.W.L.
East Horsley
April 1969

While endorsing the acknowledgments above, I should like also to express my gratitude to those other people who have made valuable contributions to the preparation of the colour drawings in this book.

I am indebted to Mr Anthony Preston of the National Maritime Museum for his enthusiastic interest and much invaluable advice. A special debt of thanks is owed to Captain K. Miyo of Japan, who, despite some personal inconvenience, was able to gather sufficient references to make it possible to draw the Japanese I 400 submarine; a last-minute disaster was thereby narrowly averted. Mr John Batchelor was unstinting with material from his own collection and was able to put me in touch with other experts. As ever I found Historical Research Unit ready with help and sound advice when things became difficult. Mr White of the Ministry of Defence (Air) helped with aircraft references and put me on to other lines of enquiry. My thanks go to Miss Tilbury of *Flight* magazine who supplied me with some excellent photographs, thus resolving an earlier crisis. Finally, here, I should like to record my gratitude to the staffs of the various libraries and museums, in this country and abroad, who gave valuable help. It seems their lot in life to remain unnamed but it is their willing co-operation and interest which contributes so much towards smoothing the researcher's stony path.

Lastly, but by no means least, I am indebted to my wife for several difficult technical translations and for her understanding in the face of the tide of books and reference material which for many months threatened to disrupt a normally well-run home.

Malcolm McGregor
June 1969

CHAPTER I

How it all began

Visitors to the Bibliothèque Royale, Brussels, can enjoy some amusing reflections from a picture in a thirteenth-century manuscript, *Le Vraie Histoire d'Alexandre*, showing this great conqueror under water in a glass barrel which has been lowered on chains to the bottom of the sea from an attendant boat on the surface.

Long before this supposed adventure the idea of navigating under water had attracted inventors, but all failed to construct a suitable vessel because they had not the material means. It was not until an Englishman, William Bourne, who had served as a gunner under the Elizabethan Admiral, Sir William Monson, had produced a treatise in the year 1580 stating exactly how ballast water could be controlled by screws operating leather bulkheads, that the possibility became a fact. Bourne's writings undoubtedly attracted the attention of Cornelius Van Drebbel, a Dutch mechanician and chemist, who adopted the ballast water principle and the idea of using leather bulkheads. Bourne said it was well known that a ship which floats displaces exactly its own weight of water. He went on to give a lucid explanation of why a ship floats and what can be done to make it 'sink or swim'.

Of the methods expounded by Bourne to make a ship do either of these things at will, Van Drebbel chose that of taking in water and discharging it again and designed a number of submarines on this principle, one of which he brought to London and demonstrated before King James I. The buoyancy of this boat could be reduced by withdrawing a leather bulkhead and taking in water through holes in the ship's side until the upper deck was awash. Then, propelled by oars, the holes for which were made watertight again by leather, the boat proceeded awash but at times completely disappeared for a few moments. Full buoyancy was recovered by screwing the leather bulkhead out to its former position.

This was considered to be very remarkable and it certainly was so for those times. There is no doubt that Van Drebbel's boat actually went from Westminster to Greenwich in this manner, but the story that King James I or even passengers went in the boat for this trip is not generally believed. Built of wood with iron frames and lined with greased leather it is said that the boat was comparatively dry inside. Being a chemist Van Drebbel improved on Bourne by introducing a chemical which circulated through the boat from an intake air pipe with the effect of purifying the air. The cycle was completed by means of bellows and an exhaust pipe. Thus an Englishman thought out the first practicable design for a submarine and a Dutchman made the first operational boat.

Van Drebbel died in 1634 and bequeathed his inventions to his son-in-law Dr Kuffler, with whom Samuel Pepys, the diarist, had 'discourses in the coffeehouse', chiefly to hear about inventions for blowing up ships, but the meeting is evidence of the interest in naval circles in England of Van Drebbel's work. Much was claimed by Bourne for his invention, such as exploring the bottom of the sea, but in the navy men reasoned that, as command of the sea was now dictated by the gun, a vessel which could submerge and thereby defeat the power of this weapon would have a great influence on sea power. However, the submarine was in such a primitive state that these very potent thoughts could not, at that time, be translated into something practical.

It was a Frenchman, de Son, who in 1653 was the first to provide mechanical power to propel a submarine. His boat, like Van Drebbel's, navigated only awash. It was 72 feet long and was fitted with an internal paddle wheel which worked in a well in the centre of the vessel. This paddle wheel was intended to be turned by a clockwork mechanism, but the power, which was sufficient when the wheel was in air, was totally inadequate when the wheel was in water. The boat was designed never to be in more than the awash position and must therefore be classed with the submersibles (ie. vessels that can submerge for brief periods) rather than with submarines proper.

From 1680 all manner of people were putting their brains to

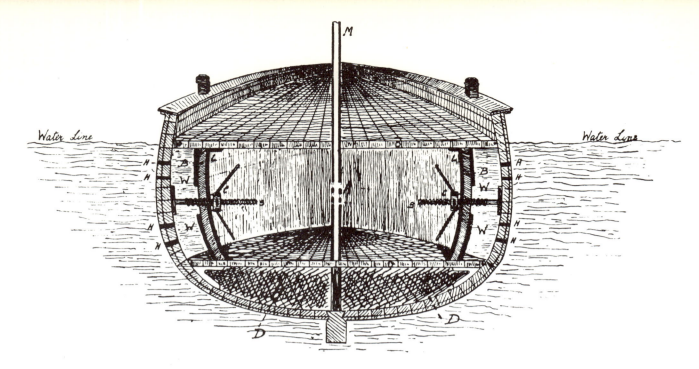

the submarine problem. This plethora of designs, and in some cases the building of actual vessels, went on until the advent of the mechanical age. To follow the development objectively it is necessary to be selective and credit must go to two French priests, Fathers Mersenne and Fournier of the Order of Minimes, who, shortly after Van Drebbel's death, produced a design for a submarine with wheels for movement along the sea bed. The boat was to have air-pumps and ventilators, phosphorescent apparatus for lighting inside, a battery of big guns to be fired on either side, with special valves to prevent the water coming in when the guns recoiled, and arrangements for a man to leave the boat submerged and return at will.

Many other inventors produced designs but none offered a true advance until the Abbé Borelli propounded a scheme for destroying the buoyancy by filling a number of leather bottles and returning to full buoyancy by expelling the water from these bottles by hand. Nevertheless no construction took place until, in 1747, an Englishman by the name of Symon built a boat. In this design he employed the idea of controlling the buoyancy by a number of leather bottles on the Borelli principle. Thus a practical step nearer the ballast tank had been taken.

Inevitably this pioneer work was dangerous and in 1773 disaster befell a ship's carpenter named Day. This man pioneered the use of detachable ballast. Large stones with ringbolts which were hung outside his submarine could be slipped from inside. Day made a successful dive in Plymouth Sound and then moved to a deeper and more exposed part of the harbour. When he got there he found his boat needed more ballast stones to make it submerge in the saltier water of the open sea and ordered more to be attached. The boat sank in 22 fathoms of water and did not reappear. It is reasonable to suppose that the pressure of water at that depth collapsed the hull. Two points emerged from Day's unfortunate experience. Firstly, had time allowed him to release his ballast he would have shot to the surface. This manoeuvre was the forerunner of devices to regain buoyancy quickly by releasing a heavy weight specially provided for this purpose. Secondly, the importance of allowing for water pressure at depth became apparent. Submarines have always been limited in their operations by this factor.

Bourne's system of ballast water control
A. *Air holes*
B. *Bulkhead which is screwed in and out*
C. *Capstan for screwing bulkhead in and out*
D. *Ballast*
H. *Inlet holes for water*
L. *Leather*
M. *Hollow mast for air supply*
W. *Space occupied by water when craft is submerged*
S. *Screws*

Below
De Son's submarine, showing internal paddle wheel

Bottom
Symon's submarine, 1747
A. Leather bottles for carrying water ballast
B. Oar aperture made watertight with leather

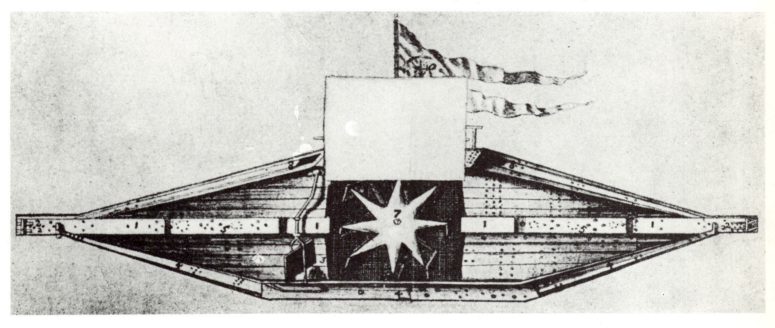

CHAPTER II

Progress through war

Progress in invention is always stimulated in wartime and the American War of Independence was no exception. David Bushnell, who graduated at Yale College in 1775, commenced there his study of the problems of a submersible vessel which he completed later. When the English blockaded the eastern seaboard in 1776 he thought that it might be possible to break this stranglehold by placing explosive charges underneath the British men-of-war – a type of weapon with which he had also been experimenting. To Bushnell's way of thinking, undoubtedly one method of carrying out this plan would be to fix the explosive charges by means of his submarine. Bushnell's boat was made of wood and shaped like two gigantic walnut shells standing on end. To strengthen it a stout piece of wood was placed across the interior so that the sides would not buckle inwards due to water pressure. This piece of wood also served as a seat for the operator. Bushnell called his submarine the *Turtle* as he considered it was shaped like one. A hole in the bottom admitted water when he wanted the boat to submerge, and two brass pumps were installed for ejecting it when he wished to surface. The operator admitted water by placing his foot on a brass valve and depressing it, and ejected it by using the pumps. On the outside of the bottom end of his *Turtle* Bushnell placed 700 lb of lead ballast, 200 lb of which could be slipped by means of a cord from inside the boat, on the lines of Day's principle, so that the operator could rise rapidly in an emergency. The boat contained enough air for one man for half an hour while submerged. When the water tank at the bottom of the boat was full the top of the *Turtle*, which had a small brass conning tower sufficiently large to contain a man's head, was just awash. This conning tower was fitted with glass windows. To go forwards or backwards Bushnell fitted an oar 'formed upon the principle of the screw' which turning one way propelled the *Turtle* forwards and the other way backwards. This oar 'screw' could be operated by either hand or foot. There was a rudder with a tiller which was long enough to be held under the operator's arm.

A second oar, again designed 'on the principle of the screw', was fitted in a vertical position near the conning tower to assist the operator to move the boat in the vertical plane. Finally, to fix the explosive charge, a small wooden screw was to be inserted into the hull of the enemy ship and released from the *Turtle* together with the explosive charge which was attached to it. By the aid of a time clock the submarine was given half an hour to escape after which the explosive went off.

Here then was a forerunner of things to come, a submersible capable of manoeuvre under its own power, submerged by means of a controlled ballast tank and armed with a weapon believed to be capable of sinking a battleship.

In 1776 the English fleet was anchored in the Hudson River and Bushnell determined to put his invention to the test. He did not man the *Turtle* himself but secured the services of a Sergeant Ezra Lee. The submarine was towed by two rowing-boats to within a few miles of the enemy and then, with the aid of the tide and the versatile Lee's efforts with the screws and tiller, it swept towards the English fleet, only to be carried past the ships by the strength of the tide. However, Lee waited in the awash position until the tide had slackened and then managed to manoeuvre his submarine, by now submerged again, under H.M.S. *Eagle*, a 64-gun two-decker ship of the line carrying the flag of Lord Howe. The attack failed only because Lee could not get the detachable screw to penetrate the copper bottom of the warship, and he gave up. When the tide turned in his favour he returned to base. On the way he was sighted by some soldiers on the shore who put out in a boat. Lee instantly slipped the detachable screw and the charge and managed to reach safety; meanwhile the time clock ran its course and the charge exploded. Later two more attempts were made but both failed and the experiment was not repeated. Nevertheless Bushnell goes down in history as the first inventor of a submarine which went into action.

One year before Ezra Lee attacked H.M.S. *Eagle* Robert

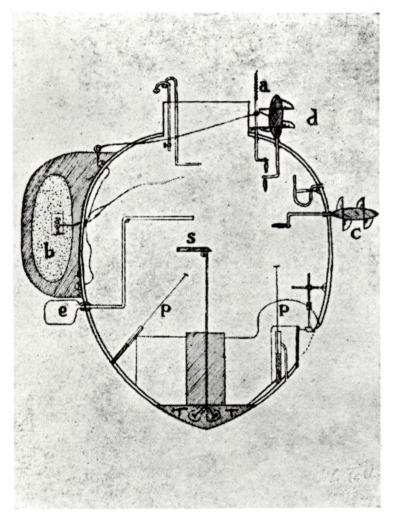

Bushnell's submarine, 1776
a. *Screw to which magazine was attached*
b. *Magazine*
c. *Screw-shaped oar for going ahead or astern*
d. *Screw-shaped oar for forcing the boat under water*
e. *Rudder*
p. *Pumps*
T. *Water ballast tanks*
s. *Seat for operator*

Fulton was born in Little Britain (now named Fulton), Pennsylvania. He was an inventor in every sense of the word. His genius led him to construct flax-spinning devices, sawmills, rope-making machines and much else. He had progressive ideas on canals and dams and was a landscape painter in his own right. His travels brought him via England to France where he found the English were this time blockading the French northern ports. Like Bushnell before him, he determined to try and break the blockade by means of a submarine carrying explosive charges. He wrote on 13th December 1797: 'Citizen Director. Having taken great interest in all that would diminish the power of the English Fleet I have planned the construction of a mechanical engine, in which I have the greatest confidence for the annihilation of this Navy.'

He went on to say that to do this he had formed 'The Nautilus Company'. He would charge the French government 4000 francs a gun for every English ship over 40 guns and proportional amounts for other ships. If the French government built their own Nautiluses this would cost them 10,000 francs for each one, payable to the inventor. As this form of attack was considered to be 'against the Laws of War' he asked for arrangements to be made that any man captured during these operations should be considered to be a prisoner of war and not hung or otherwise put to death.

These first proposals were turned down by the French so he approached the Dutch government, who also rejected them. Not too depressed, Fulton returned to France and made a personal approach to Bonaparte who licensed a grant of 10,000 francs of public money to enable Fulton to make a start with his first boat. She was laid down in 1800 and completed in the same year. The submarine was 21 feet 4 inches long and 7 feet in diameter. The hull was made of copper with iron frames. Like Bushnell's *Turtle* there was a detachable keel which could be slipped in an emergency. Water ballast was admitted into tanks and a double pump was fitted to discharge it. She was considered strong enough to go to 25 feet in depth. For the first time in submarine development horizontal hydroplanes were fitted aft. A further innovation was the anchor gear which could be let go from inside the boat. Motive power was provided by a two-bladed propeller in the stern which was turned by hand. On the surface it was intended that the boat would manoeuvre by sail for which there was a collapsible mast stowed on the upper deck when the submarine was dived. To work the boat there was a crew of three men.

Fulton's *Nautilus* was as near to something really practicable in submarine design as anyone could go in his day and age. The introduction of hydroplanes to help the vessel maintain even depth and the fitting of a propeller were great advances. It can be said, further, that this was the first submarine to have two sources of motive power. The striking-power against an enemy was similar to Bushnell's except that Fulton employed a strong spike for driving into the bottom of the hull of a ship, and to this the explosive charge was attached by a stout line. The explosive was fired by means of a lanyard and gunlock instead of a clockwork device.

Fulton first demonstrated his *Nautilus* on 13th June 1800 opposite the Hotel des Invalides between the present Concorde and Alma bridges. Other dives took place at Rouen and Le Havre in July and August. Later *Nautilus* was stationed at Brest and dived successfully in the open sea. These diving tests were witnessed with considerable astonishment. Finally an old schooner was placed at his disposal which he blew up by towing an explosive charge underneath. This was towed by a barge but it showed the possibilities for use by a submarine.

Eventually Fulton was allowed to try and sink one or more of the English frigates off Brest but he never got near enough to them to fix his charge.

Finally Fulton's plans had a mixed reception in high circles because of the moral objection to this kind of warfare. Admiral Pleville le Pelley, for example, who had been Minister of Marine in 1798, declared that his conscience would not allow him to have recourse to so terrible an invention. On the other hand Monsieur Forfait, a prominent Naval Constructor, was enthusiastic.

Before going home to America Fulton decided on one more try in England and in 1804 laid his plans before the British government. Pitt, then Prime Minister, was attracted by the demonstrations but Admiral Earl St Vincent, then First Lord of the Admiralty, while recognising Fulton's inventive genius said with great emphasis, 'Pitt was the greatest fool that ever existed to encourage a mode of warfare which those who commanded the seas did not want, and which, if successful, would deprive them of it.' This profound statement was to influence British naval affairs for the next hundred years and more, and is itself sufficient to justify Fulton's name being added to the list of those who contributed to the development of this underwater weapon.

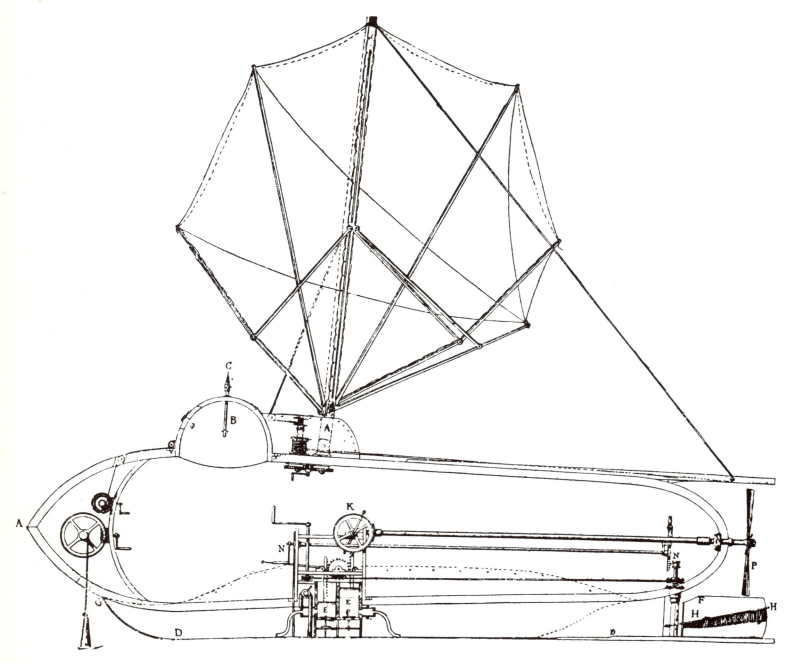

Fulton's NAUTILUS, 1800
A. Mast
B. Conning tower
C. Spike for putting into the bottom of a hostile ship
D. Keel
E. Kingston valves
F. Vertical rudder
G. Anchor
H. Inclined plane diving rudders
K. Hand wheel for rotating propeller (P)
N. Gearing for working vertical rudder

CHAPTER III

Enter the mechanical age

During the first half of the nineteenth century, when the beginnings of the mechanical age were making their mark on naval affairs, submarine development made little progress until 1850 when a Bavarian, William Bauer, built the first iron submarine. Bauer was inspired from the same motives as Bushnell and Fulton, namely naval blockade. This time Germany and Denmark were at war and the superior Danish fleet was blockading the German seaboard.

Bauer's submarine was $26\frac{1}{2}$ feet long and had a displacement of $38\frac{1}{2}$ tons. Symon's principle for submerging by taking in ballast water as developed by Bushnell and Fulton was now fully accepted, so this boat was fitted with tanks with inlet valves in double bottoms for destroying the buoyancy and pumps for discharging the water. Having brought the boat to a state of equilibrium with the upper deck awash, Bauer moved a heavy weight which gave the boat an inclination. As soon as she started to go under he moved it back and so the boat submerged in a succession of dips. This was different from Van Drebbel's oars and Bushnell's vertical screws, and did not rely on Fulton's principle of forward motion by propeller and horizontal stability by hydroplanes, although Bauer had a propeller at the stern which was hand-operated. He also had an explosive charge for securing to the bottom of an enemy ship, the difference between it and Fulton's being that it was fired by an electric battery.

Bauer made a feint at the Danish ships and this had the desired effect of making them lie off at a respectful distance. The submarine's influence was growing. While this development itself made history in the sphere of naval operations it was on the technical side where Bauer also made his name. On 1st February 1851, when off Kiel, Bauer and two seamen dived in the submarine but, on reaching the deepest part of the harbour, the sheet iron hull began to give way and water came in. The boat sank to the bottom out of control in 54 feet of water. Bauer kept his head and ordered his men to let in more water so that the whole interior was flooding. The two seamen, terrified, refused to obey but Bauer managed, even in this desperate situation, to convince them that this was their only hope of survival. Indeed the danger now came more from the anchors and grapnels which those on the surface threw down in an effort to grasp the boat and raise it. In due time the water entering the boat compressed the air inside to such an extent that the pressure inside equalled that of the water outside and, without any aid from Bauer, the weakly constructed hatch flew open, releasing the bubble of air and taking Bauer and his two companions with it. They had been down five hours and had made the first free escape from a sunken submarine.

In common with other pioneers Bauer was discredited in his own country and, after some time spent in England where his brains were tapped but he was not employed, he persuaded the Russians to let him build a submarine. The result was a submarine similar to the first but bigger, being 52 feet long and with a beam of 12 feet. The boat was launched in 1855, and a year later, during the coronation of Alexander II on 6th September 1854, he took several musicians with him and submerged to the harbour bed. When the guns began the Royal Salute his band struck up with the National Anthem. This lark was not without its technical aspect, as the ships in harbour heard the strains of music, and although Bauer himself had already been interested in the rising science of underwater sound waves his novel idea gave impetus to the subject.

It was now that the French, following in the wake of de Son and the Abbé Borelli, began to take a major interest in submarines. Their contribution which followed has not, in the opinion of many, been fully recognised outside their own country.

In 1858 Captain (later Vice Admiral) Bourgois designed 'Le projet du Plongeur'. This was examined by officers of the Corps of Naval Constructors, and the development was recommended by Brun, a naval Commander and member of the Corps of Constructors (later Director of Naval Construction). The design was accepted and the keel was laid in June 1860. This boat was 140 feet long and displaced 420 tons. The propulsion was by compressed air which drove a propeller. The engine was designed by Brun. The submarine was made of iron plates fastened to a heavy keel which extended right forward to support the spar which carried the explosive charge—an ambitious project.

In a hollow part of the hull a salvage boat was fitted, capable of taking twelve men. The boat was bolted to the hull and pressure inside the submarine was kept just above that of the water outside so that there was no seepage of water at the bolts into the vessel.

The *Plongeur* had trouble. She was fitted with a system of moving water from one end of the boat to the other by means of pipes and pistons to control the longitudinal equilibrium. This system worked too slowly so that the boat plunged about. The hydroplanes in the stern were found to have insufficient power to eliminate this so a vertical screw was added. This did not cure the trouble. Besides this difficulty, naval officers considered that the explosive, which was carried on a spar in the bow, was too weak to justify further development of the submarine weapon at that stage. Nevertheless she was the first submarine which did not rely on human power for propulsion. The year was 1863.

It is necessary to leave the French development for a brief period at this point because at this time, in the New World, America was in a state of civil war and by 1864 the north, having built up their naval forces, set about blockading the south. For the third time this form of naval warfare made its impact on the development of the submarine. Both sides had built ironclads and the famous fight between the Federal *Monitor* and the Confederate *Virginia* had already revolutionised naval thinking. But more than this, the Confederates were the first to appreciate that the submarine was to be the weapon of the weaker power and they built their 'Davids'. This biblical name was the obvious choice for a submarine designed to attack an ironclad. The 'Davids' were not proper submarines as they could only 'trim down', thereby reducing their silhouettes to a minimum. Some were propelled by hand and others by steam. One steam *David* damaged the Federal armed ship *Ironsides*, and another, hand propelled, sank the wooden *Housatonic* by charging the ship with its bow explosive which opened a hole in the engine room but at the same time sank the *David* with all hands. It is not without significance that this particular *David* had been sunk while exercising no less than three times, with considerable loss of life, due to total lack of experience, more particularly operating in the awash condition with the hatches open. But each time new crews were forthcoming. The navies of the world followed these events with the greatest interest and noted that when the victorious Federals overran the Confederate dockyards they found a full-scale submarine programme under way. Weaker naval powers took careful note of the possibilities open to them through the development of the submarine, while Britain pondered on the words of Lord St Vincent.

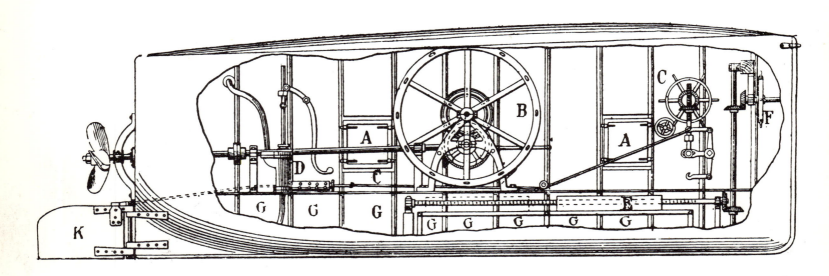

Bourgois's PLONGEUR, 1860
A. Hatches for crew to enter by
B. Hand-wheel for rotating the propeller
C. Steering wheel and rods to rudder (K)
D. Pump for ejecting water ballast
E. Heavy weight for altering longitudinal trim
F. Gearing for moving weight (E)
G. Water ballast tanks

Opposite page
The Confederate 'Davids', c. 1865
a & b: A steam 'David'
c, d & e: A hand-propelled 'David'
(Hydroplanes are marked X)
f: The spar torpedo of a 'David'
(the chemical fuses for exploding the charge are marked N)

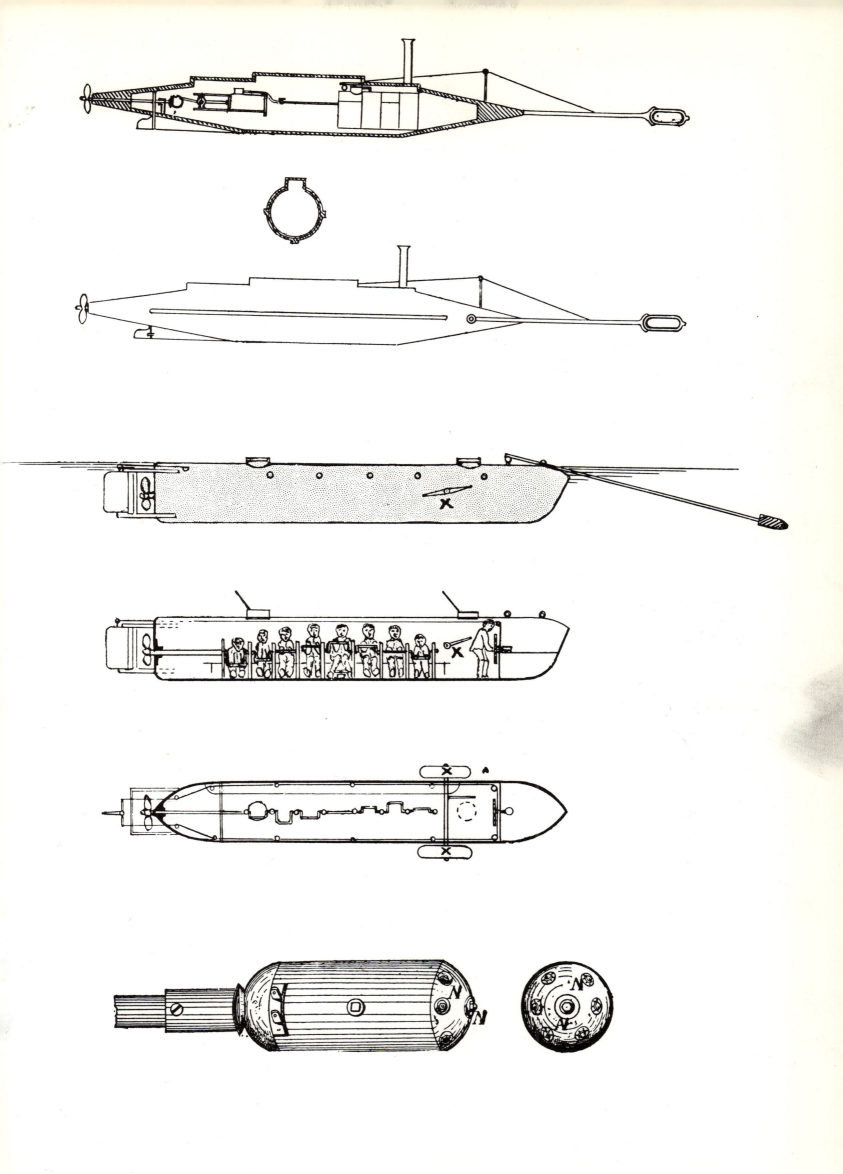

CHAPTER IV

Introduction to the Twentieth Century: France and America show the way

Some fifteen years later a notable development took place in France. This was not surprising since France had always been in the lead in naval construction in Europe, particularly at the height of the sailing ship era. Monsieur Claude Goubet, a civil engineer, designed two submarines, the *Goubet I* and *II*. Both were very small, one idea being that such a boat could be hoisted on board a battleship and used as an invisible torpedo boat. Only 16½ feet in length and weighing 11 tons *Goubet I* was propelled by electric power from a battery of Laurent-Cély accumulators. She was provided with a small periscope. A circular hole in the bows allowed a steel bar to be run out about 10 feet which carried a scissor device for cutting enemy nets. This boat was built in Paris and took the water on the Seine for the first time on 20th March 1887. Trials were run in October 1888, after which she was sent to Cherbourg where, between 1889 and 1892, she was set an agreed programme but did not succeed in completing it, being unsteady both in course and diving depth, with the result that the Minister of Marine refused to accept her.

The second *Goubet*, 26 feet long, was also built on the Seine, this time at Agenteuil. Unhappily she was unsuccessful for much the same reasons as *Goubet I*, and when the French Navy tried her out in 1899 at Toulon she, too, was not accepted. Nevertheless, had she succeeded in her trials the proposal was to fit her with two torpedoes, to be launched from dropping gear. Thus the first submarine fitted with electric power and designed to carry torpedoes never entered service, but credit must go to Goubet for his part in the story of the evolution of the submarine.

It must not be supposed that by this time there had been no other submarines constructed or designed than those mentioned in this book. On the contrary, this process of development had been going on ever since Van Drebbel's day, but large numbers of submarines, attributed to designers all over the world, never got further than the drawing board, and those which were completed, some of which were quite important, have not been specifically mentioned as it is considered that the submarines which have been named and described contributed the most to overall development.

Between Van Drebbel and the end of the nineteenth century somewhere between 130 and 140 designs for submarines are known to have received serious consideration, and upwards of 50 others were both designed and built, some of which were successful within the limits of the materials and scientific knowledge available in their day.

Some of the ideas put forward in the designs were most ingenious, ranging from a railway on the bottom of the sea, to boats with special doors in their bottoms to allow divers to leave the submarine temporarily to examine the sea bed. Except that they were better educated than most other people, it is curious how interested men in Holy Orders seemed to be in submarine design. Perhaps the Protestant Church felt that all the honours should not go to the Abbé Borelli. Whatever the reason, the Reverend Garrett, an Englishman, designed a submarine in 1878 and followed this a few years later with his *Resurgam*. Garrett unfortunately was unable to develop his ideas without help, and turned to Mr Nordenfeldt, a Swedish gun-maker who accepted Garrett's general ideas and, adding his own, produced three workable designs during the next eight years. These boats were built by the Naval Construction and Armament Company at Barrow-in-Furness. Two were sold to Greece and Turkey where it was found they were too difficult to operate submerged. A third was sold to Russia, but this one foundered on the surface on passage. The French attended the trials of these boats, but did not like them. They were steam-driven and gave speeds of 14 knots on the surface and 5–8 knots submerged, using reserve steam in tanks stored internally. *Nordenfeldt III* achieved a marked advance with two internal torpedo tubes.

Had this design been taken up by the British government progress might have been made which would have produced an advanced type of submarine in the British Navy, but the

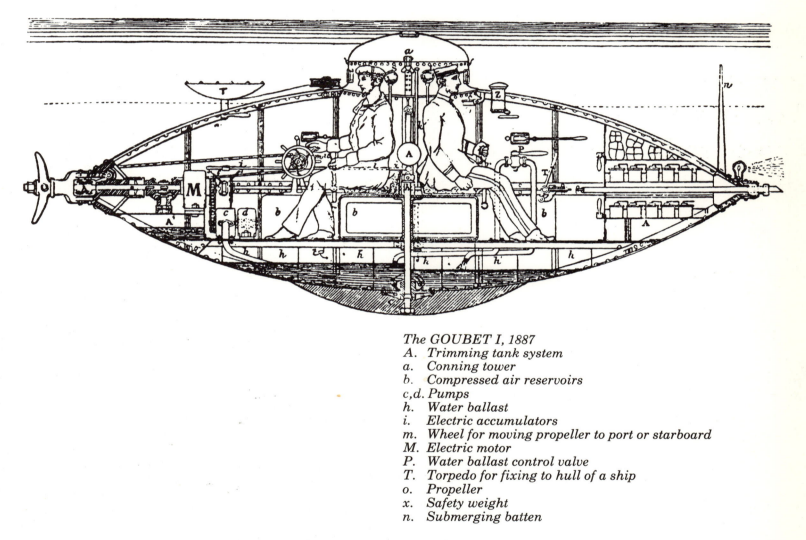

The GOUBET I, 1887
A. Trimming tank system
a. Conning tower
b. Compressed air reservoirs
c,d. Pumps
h. Water ballast
i. Electric accumulators
m. Wheel for moving propeller to port or starboard
M. Electric motor
P. Water ballast control valve
T. Torpedo for fixing to hull of a ship
o. Propeller
x. Safety weight
n. Submerging batten

advocates of the submarine in Britain were outnumbered by the sceptics and nothing was done.

During the eight years in which Nordenfeldt was building his boats, other French designers besides Goubet were not idle. A retired Naval Constructor, Monsieur Zédé, set about collating all the best plans available to him from French Constructors. From this research he produced the *Gymnote*, in which the distinctive feature was the discharging of ballast water by compressed air. At this time the French Minister of Marine was Admiral Aube, who fully appreciated the potentialities of the *Gymnote*, and, brushing aside the prejudices of the old school of naval officers, gave the first government order for the construction of a submarine.

This was a period when French designers with their forward thinking on submarine matters were some ten years ahead of their contemporaries in other nations. Most prominent in this field was Monsieur Dupuy de Lôme, a celebrated French engineer. His was the inspiration behind the *Gymnote* and its first designer, but he died in 1885. However, Gustave Zédé completed the plans and supervised the construction, which was carried out at Toulon by his nephew, Romazotti, then a young Naval Constructor. The *Gymnote* was only 60 feet long and of 31 tons displacement, but Admiral Aube considered this would be a suitable size for coast defence and pioneered the idea that the submarine could replace much of the defensive mining which was common practice at that time. At first *Gymnote* was fitted with hydroplanes aft only, but when in 1890 the French Navy took over the boat her Commanding Officer, Lieutenant Darriens (later Vice Admiral) advised two additional pairs of hydroplanes. These were later reduced to two pairs in all. Eventually *Gymnote* was given an extensive refit in 1897–98 and provided with a new motor, a variable-pitch propeller, a new battery with lead accumulators, and two dropping gears for 14-inch torpedoes. She was never put to operational use but was invaluable as a trials boat and was not scrapped until May 1908.

In 1890 Romazotti himself submitted a new design incorporating all that was best in the *Gymnote*. Gustave Zédé died during the construction of this second boat, which was named after him. To assist better depth-keeping, hydroplanes were fitted midships as well as aft and forward, but the most striking improvement was the automatic bow cap which shut immediately a torpedo was fired. The torpedoes were 17 feet 7 inches long, but the change in balance or trim on firing could be well held by the three pairs of hydroplanes. To meet what were considered to be naval requirements of

De Lôme's and Zédé's GYMNOTE, launched at Toulon in 1888

sea-keeping and habitability the *Gustave Zédé* was 148 feet long and displaced 266 tons.

On reflection this was considered rather too big a jump in size, but in spite of difficulties the French persevered with her and made her into a sound operational submarine. Meanwhile, in 1896 the French Minister of Marine, Monsieur Lockrey, had organised a competition in response to which six complete designs were submitted. The winner was Monsieur Laubeuf with his design for the *Narval* (Plate I). The requirements were 200 tons displacement with a radius of action on the surface of 100 miles at 12 knots, and 10 miles at 8 knots when submerged. To meet the surface radius requirement Laubeuf provided steam propulsion, and employed electric battery power for submerged propulsion only, thus introducing the two-power system to Europe. Other advances were a double hull, the space between the two hulls being used for ballast water and for a system of tanks to compensate for various weights carried and consumed, such as fuel for the engines and food for the crew. The *Narval* was 111 feet long and displaced 168 tons. The range of action on the surface was 250 miles at 11 knots and 500 miles at 7.5 knots. Submerged, her batteries gave 25 miles at 6 knots and 75 miles at 5 knots. Laubeuf had definite operational requirements in mind and visualised his submarine leaving Brest or Cherbourg at night and crossing the channel on the surface for diving operations off Plymouth, Portsmouth or the Thames. The *Narval* was fully capable of fulfilling these objects. As early as 1901 she successfully forced the difficult entrance of the Brest roadstead after cruising for 48 hours in Channel. She and her sister submarines remained the undoubted leaders in submarine capability until 1905. By 1899 the French had made up their minds that the submarine was definitely the weapon of the future, and within a year produc-ed a plan to build a submarine fleet of 39 boats partly of 'Gustave Zédé' type with electric propulsion only and partly of 'Narval' type with the two-power propulsion system.

Across the Atlantic meanwhile, one man had dominated the advance in submarine design. This man was Mr John P. Holland of Paterson, New Jersey. From 1875 to 1887 Holland designed seven submarines. They were of varying sizes and met with varying fortunes, from disaster and shipwreck to never getting further than the drawing board, but when, in 1887, Mr Whitney, Secretary of the Navy, invited designs for a submarine, Holland's designs had reached No. VII. This he submitted to the Navy Bureau and it was accepted. The boat was planned with the two-power system of propulsion, thus introducing this method to the New World. Holland experimented with types of petrol engine instead of steam, and these were quite successful.

Whitney had in mind some alternative to the vulnerability of torpedo boats to surface gunfire. A large number of designs were sent in, and three were accepted to be taken a stage further. They were the Baker boat, the Lake boat and Holland's, all named after their designers.

Baker's boat failed on trials because the propelling system, which was linked to the diving system, prevented an even depth line being held.

That Lake's design was not finally accepted by the United States Navy in no way deterred this undaunted designer, and he went ahead with his *Argonaut I* and *II*, concentrating on a submersible which could go along the sea bed on wheels and from which divers could make explorations. Within its limitations *Argonaut II* was successful, and following this the *Protector* was built and armed with three torpedoes. The United States Navy Board considered this submarine very good for harbour defence and an improvement on mining,

besides which they liked her ability to accommodate divers for cutting cables and other work on the sea bed. Much play was made of the fact that she could be connected with the shore by telephone, and that there were flat surfaces of the sea bed off the eastern seaboard running out as far as 175 miles suitable for *Argonaut II*.

'Holland VII', which the Navy Bureau accepted, was the subject of a good deal of wrangling in high places, and the contract was not signed until 1895. Further delays occurred, and it was not until 23rd June 1896 that the keel was laid down. On 27th August 1897 she was launched under the name of *Plunger*. Holland was obliged by the Navy Bureau to adopt steam propulsion for surface running, fitting two triple-expansion engines driving two propellers. The considerable steam power which the naval authorities attempted made the boat unhabitable on account of the high temperature, and completion was abandoned for some considerable time. This influenced John Holland to form the Holland Boat Company.

Meanwhile, Holland built his No. VIII privately in his own company's yard. The boat was an undoubted success, and Holland placed her at the disposal of the naval authorities, who bought her. Thus a submarine entered the United States Navy some ten years after the French had taken this memorable step with the *Gymnote*. She was 53 feet long, 6 feet shorter than *Gymnote*, and of 75 tons displacement, that is to say, double the size. Abandoning steam, Holland placed his faith in his petrol engines for surface running. There was one torpedo tube forward and she carried one reload. In this boat lay the prototype of submarines of the United States and Great Britain for the next fifty years. In June 1900 Congress ordered the construction of six boats of improved surface and submerged performance ('Holland IX'), the first of which was christened *Adder*.

Before the century ended a number of other countries had taken positive action in submarine navigation, but none had made any important contribution to the evolution of the submarine. In Spain a young lieutenant, Isaac Peral, designed a boat which was launched in 1887 and was fairly successful. She was of all-electric propulsion and had two propellers. With a length of 70 feet and of 80 tons displacement she compared closely with Holland's boats, but Peral gave her vertical screws for depth-keeping, following the Nordenfeldt principle, and this inhibited acceptance by the Spanish government. In the event, a Royal Commission decided, after the most exhaustive study of all available information on submarines, not to proceed with further construction. They did, however, reward Peral handsomely for this work.

Russia's contribution was centred on their inventor Drzewiecki, who came second to Laubeuf in the French competition and designed special 'drop collars' for launching torpedoes carried externally. Italy had come to no definite policy with the submarine as a weapon of war. Meanwhile Germany was holding her hand, believing to some extent that the shallow waters around her coast gave ample protection to her ports at least for the time being, and influenced by Admiral Tirpitz's policy to build up a battle fleet at all costs. The Japanese were just watchful, and this can also be said for the Portuguese. In Sweden they had the great experience of Nordenfeldt, but moved on to building a submarine named the *Hajem* on the Holland design with a petrol engine for surface propulsion, and in Holland itself there were plans for building a boat on the design of their namesake. Austria was in much the same position. That the new century would be a momentous one in the evolution of the submarine was certain.

The GUSTAVE ZEDE, c. 1890, running at full speed

CHAPTER V

Acceptance by the Navies of the World

The year 1900 can be taken as the dividing line between the age of technical experiment and reality since in the next decade the submarine was to take its place fully in the navies of the world.

Six navies now possessed a total of ten submarines and there were another eleven under construction. In numbers France was well in the lead with a total of fourteen built and building. She was concentrating on steam for surface propulsion because of troubles with early internal combustion engines which had proved difficult to resolve. On the other hand America, with only two submarines, was set fair for the future. Although the petrol engine of the 'Holland' was far from perfect and indeed could be dangerous, its selection for surface propulsion was only one step from the shape of things to come, namely the diesel. Both countries used electric motors for submerged propulsion and it was clear that this method had come to stay. The Whitehead torpedo, common to both countries' designs, was assured of its future as the primary weapon for firing from either external or internal torpedo tubes.

Great Britain so far had no submarines and was clinging now by tender threads to the Lord St Vincent doctrine. In Germany Admiral Tirpitz had determined to build a battle fleet of sufficient strength to challenge British supremacy, and played down the submarine on the grounds that the German Navy would wait and see if this untried new warship had a future or not.

During 1901 the French still pressed ahead. Already they were experimenting with solid injection engines for surface propulsion. More impressive, however, in their manoeuvres that year was the submersible *Gustave Zédé* which attacked the French fleet leaving Ajaccio and 'torpedoed' the battleship *Charles Martel*. Here was something of major naval significance—the submarine could be a weapon of attack and, moreover, could operate unsupported.

The British government therefore could no longer disregard this danger, and on the excuse that the only way to be efficient in anti-submarine technique was to possess the vessel and study it at first hand, made the decision to introduce submarines into the British Navy.

'Close attention has been given by the Admiralty to the subject of submarine boats.' Viscount Goschen, First Lord of the Admiralty, had made this statement in April 1900. Now, one year later, his successor Lord Selborne announced: 'Five submarine vessels of the type invented by Mr Holland have been ordered, the first of which should be delivered next autumn. What the future value of these boats may be in naval warfare can only be a matter of conjecture, but experiments with these boats will assist the Admiralty in assessing their true value.'

Already, however, the pattern was taking shape in the minds of the world's naval leaders. It was clear that the smallest type could replace some of the defensive mining of harbours. A slightly larger type could influence blockading ships to keep their distance and possibly bring about the lifting of a blockade altogether. In the double motive-power large boats there was a potential attacking force, capable of operating unseen and unsupported against the enemy's coast and sea communications.

The five British 'Hollands' (Plate II), which were all built at the works of Messrs Vickers, Son and Maxim at Barrow-in-Furness, in England, did not begin their lives too happily. During construction both the builders and the naval representative, Captain R. N. Bacon, became convinced that there must be something wrong with the drawings, and it was decided to send for an American naval officer to advise. He, too, was certain the drawings were wrong, but the authorities at the top decided that construction must continue. It was not until *Holland I* was undergoing trials in the dock and nearly turned on end that the modifications recommended were carried out and all was well. So well, in fact, that in a few years Britain was leading the field.

The British 'Hollands', in spite of the modifications, were

almost identical to those of the United States. They were found to control well at all speeds. They carried two officers and five ratings. No periscope was supplied, so Captain Bacon produced his own design.

It must not be thought that these first five British submarines did not have their troubles after leaving the builders' yard. An early test of their capabilities was a surface trip from Portsmouth round the Isle of Wight. All five boats started together, but three were out of action by the time they got to the Spit Fort, which is only a mile or so from the entrance to the main harbour. One broke down about half-way to the well-known yachting centre at Cowes, and the fifth finally came to grief directly opposite the Royal Yacht Squadron Club House. In time these difficulties were successfully overcome, and from the 'Hollands' Britain designed her own first submarine, *A.1*.

It was *Le Matin* which now took a hand in helping the French Navy to advance further in submarine construction, by running a national subscription which raised 300,000 francs. This was presented to the nation for the construction of two submarine boats. They were built from designs of Romazotti. The first, the *Français*, was launched at Cherbourg in January 1901, and the second, named *Algérien*, in February of the following year. These were single motive-power boats with electric propulsion and single propellers and were 118 feet long with surface displacement of 143 tons, thoroughly manageable craft and efficient for their purpose of coast defence.

From this date until 1905 French submarine building, while contributing a considerable amount to the evolution of the submarine, was so varied that the exact nature of the contribution is difficult to evaluate. Under the chaotic policy of Monsieur Pelletan, Minister of Marine, France built a variety of submersibles ranging from the very small up to 800 tons displacement. Some were entirely electric-propelled, one was driven by a heavy-oil engine for both surface and submerged running. Others had gasoline engines of various types. The heavy-oil engine was never a success because of the difficulty of providing air when submerged, and the petrol engines were so dangerous that they were eventually banned altogether by the Minister of Marine. It is hardly surprising that with such constant chopping and changing no standard type emerged, but the exercising which was carried out, particularly by the 'Narval' class, enabled the French not only to define clearly the roles of their submarine force in harbour and coast defence but also to point the way to the 'overseas' submarine of the future.

It was in 1904 that Britain, through the dynamic vision of Admiral Sir John Fisher (Jackie Fisher), caught up and overtook French thinking. The following letter sums up the position in 1904 so well that it is reproduced in full. Admiral Fisher was Commander-in-Chief Portsmouth at this time.

Admiralty House,
Portsmouth.
April 20th, 1904.

My dear friend,

I will begin with the last thing in your letter, which is far the most important, and that is our paucity of submarines. I consider it the most serious thing at present affecting the British Empire. That sounds big, but it is true. Had either the Russians or the Japanese had submarines the whole face of their war would have been changed for both sides. It really makes me laugh to read of Admiral Togo's eighth attack on Port Arthur! Why! Had he possessed submarines it would have been all over with the whole Russian Fleet caught like rats in a trap. Similarly, the Japanese Admiral Togo outside would never have dared to let his transports, full of troops, persue the even tenor of their way to Chemulpo and elsewhere!

It is astounding to me, perfectly astounding, how the very best amongst us fail to realize the vast impending revolution in Naval warfare and Naval strategy that the submarine will accomplish! (I have written a paper on this but it is so violent that I am keeping it!). Here, at Portsmouth, just to take a single instance, is the battleship *Empress of India* engaged on manoeuvres and knowing of the proximity of submarines, the Flagship of the Second Admiral of the Home Fleet, nine miles beyond the Nab Light (out in the open) so self-confident of safety and so oblivious to the possibilities of modern warfare that the Admiral is smoking his cigarette, the Captain is calmly seeing defaulters on the half-deck, no one caring an iota for what is going on, and suddenly they see a Whitehead torpedo miss their stern by a few feet! And how fired? From a submarine of the 'pre-Adamite' period, small, slow, badly fitted, *with no periscope at all*, and yet this submarine followed that battleship for a solid two hours under water, coming up gingerly about a mile off every now and then like a beaver! Just to take a fresh compass bearing on her prey and then down again.

Remember that this is done (and I want specially to emphasize the point) with a Lieutenant in command of the boat out in her for the first time in his life on his own account, and half the crew never out before either. Why, it is wonderful! And so what results may we expect when bigger and faster boats and periscopes more powerful than the naked eye (such as the latest pattern one I saw the other day) and with experienced Officers and crews and with nests of the submarines acting together?

I have not disguised my opinion in season and out of season as to the essential, imperative, immediate, vital, pressing, urgent (I cannot think of any more adjectives) necessity for more submarines at once – at the very least twenty-five in addition to those now ordered and building and 100 more as soon as practicable, or we shall be caught with our breeches down just as the Russians have been!

And then, my dear friend, you have the astounding audacity to say to me: 'I presume you only think they (the submarines) can act on the defensive'!! Why, my dear fellow, not take the offensive? Good Lord! If our Admiral is worth his salt he will tow his submarines at eighteen knot speed and put them into the hostile port (like ferrets after the rabbits) before war is officially declared. Just as the Japanese acted before the Russian Naval Officers knew that war was declared.

In all seriousness I don't think it is even faintly realized the immense, impending revolution which the submarine will effect as offensive weapons of war.

When you calmly sit down and work out what will happen in the narrow waters of the Channel and the Mediterranean – how totally the submarines will alter the effect of Gibraltar, Port Said, Lemnos and Malta, it makes one's hair stand on end.

Yours,
J. A. FISHER

Within a short space of time Admiral Fisher became First Sea Lord and set himself to following up his thoughts on submarines. Classes 'B' and 'C' followed in quick succession and both made cruises around the English coast in a flotilla numbering seventeen boats. These led to the construction of *D.1* which proved to the world that the submarine would definitely have a major influence on sea power. *D.1* was laid down in 1906 and completed in 1908 and was the first British submarine fitted with diesel engines, thus ending for this country the petrol-engine era. Experimental diesel engines had been fitted in British submarines as far back as *A.13*, but no whole class of submarines had been constructed with this type of propulsion. *D.1* had far better endurance than any previous boats, having a range of 2500 miles, and could do a steady 14½ knots on the surface at full speed. Submerged, her batteries could provide power for short bursts of 10 knots. She was the first British submarine with twin screws. Her ballast tanks were not inside the hull but fitted on the outside as 'saddle tanks', a principle which was to be followed intensively for half a century.

Because of her size she was given one stern torpedo tube since it was thought that it might not be possible always to turn such a large boat quickly enough to bring the bow tubes to bear. The advantages of the 'D' class were capped by the fitting of wireless for the first time. In these vessels the 'overseas' submarine became a reality.

CHAPTER VI

World Wars

By 1914 over one hundred and thirty years had passed since Bushnell attacked the British fleet in the Hudson River. During this time the pattern of the submarine as a fighting ship had been established from the technical aspect, but its evolution as far as naval operations were concerned had progressed mostly on paper, in the writings of naval officers, and little advance had been made in practice.

When the First World War broke out the Germans, under Admiral von Tirpitz, had twenty-five operational submarines. Their task was to carry out a war of attrition against the British Grand Fleet, with the object of reducing it to parity with the German High Seas Fleet, so that a major fleet action could be fought at the will of the Germans with a reasonable chance of success. The presence of these few German submarines in the North Sea and the eastern approaches to the English Channel, and the sinking by *U.9* of the three British armoured cruisers *Hogue*, *Aboukir* and *Cressey*, made the Grand Fleet move from its base at Scapa Flow to harbours on the west coast of Scotland until anti-submarine measures had been worked up. When *U.20* actually made the north-about passage to the west coast of the British Isles in a voyage of eighteen days (the passage of the Dover Straits was by now too dangerous) the Grand Fleet again took heed, and when at sea only moved at high speed and zigzagged.

Thus in the space of a few months the submarine could hardly have done more to influence naval operations. This rapid evolution could well have stopped here, at least for the time being, but when the German naval staff heard from the Army Command, somewhat unexpectedly, that the war was likely to be a long one, it was decided to attack commerce. This decision posed a major problem. The German 'U' boats had exceeded all expectations in their capabilities of endurance and hitting power, but what they could not do without endangering themselves to an unacceptable degree was to visit and search in accordance with international law and in so doing abandon their greatest asset, namely, submergence.

Thus unrestricted warfare against commerce gradually came into being both because of its potential to win the war at sea, which the army could not do on land, and because of the submarine's vulnerability when not acting in its true element.

As the war dragged on into years instead of the originally expected months, there were many intermittent periods when the Germans eased their attack on commerce, depending on the fluctuation of international opinion. They also built the first submarine merchant ship which, in 1916, visited United States ports, demonstrating that the British blockade of German commerce could be broken by this method. The first of class was named *Deutschland* (Plate IV) and made a favourable impression on the Americans. However, after the stalemate of the battle fleets following the battle of Jutland, and the sinking of the *Lusitania* which brought America into the war on 6th April 1917, the submarine became for the first time the main weapon of a major sea power. In so doing it had evolved from a coastal defence intelligent mine to a primary warship.

During the period 1915 to mid-1917, 104 German operational submarines, out of a total strength of 148, sank over three and a half million tons of shipping, two million of which was British, and defeat for England was a mere six weeks away. At this point not only was the submarine the major weapon of German sea power but it had nearly brought the greatest sea power in the world to defeat.

Typical of these submarines was *U.35* (Plate III), commanded by Von Arnaud de la Perière, a German submarine ace, who sank over a quarter of a million tons of shipping in the Mediterranean.

By mid summer 1917 German 'U' boats were not only making the long passage to the Mediterranean without difficulty but were also reaping a harvest across the Atlantic on the eastern American seaboard. Among the submarines used were the large merchant boats converted to the 'U.151' class which, armed with 5.9-inch guns and carrying twenty-two torpedoes, could stay at sea for three months.

Naturally anti-submarine measures took the highest priority in the British Navy, but apart from the introduction of the convoy system, which virtually saved England, scientific measures such as the Hydrophone had been singularly ineffective and there was nothing being developed on which any great hopes could be pinned.

Nevertheless, the submarine had not yet replaced the battleship as the primary ship in the navies of the world, but a place was found for it within the battle fleet itself in the British Navy. Great Britain built the 'K' class (Plate V) which were three times the size and of seven times the horse-power of any former British submarine. Two flotillas of these magnificent boats were formed to operate with the Grand Fleet, for which they needed a speed of 24 knots, achieved comfortably through the Parsons steam turbine. No opportunity came their way to put their tactics with the fleet into practice but they accompanied the fleet until the end of the war and were unique in the evolution of the submarine.

To summarise the position at the end of the war it can be said that basically the submarine did not alter. Submarines were merely larger and improved in many ways. For example, some submarines carried ten torpedo tubes instead of six but the two-power propulsion system remained. On the operational side both the two major sea powers had found the submarine ineffective for defence. For instance, none of the German raids on the English coast had been intercepted by submarines although considerable numbers had been reserved for this purpose. Again, rather than replacing the mine, submarines were used by both sides for the purpose of mine-laying, particularly the Germans with their 'U.C' class, which were the first to adapt mines for laying by means of the torpedo tubes.

What transcended all other considerations was the proved ability to operate unsupported against the enemy's coasts and in the oceans. Through the world-shattering employment of unrestricted warfare, which allowed full use of the torpedo unseen instead of the surface use of the gun, the submarine was making full use of its property of submergence and its powerful weapon, the torpedo. For good measure the mere presence of the submarine in the oceans had a marked influence on fleets which was often simply psychological.

These advances in the operational sphere of naval warfare brought the submarine to a position where its defeat of a major sea power was a possibility. In all, German submarines sank 5708 ships totalling over 11 million tons and equalling one quarter of the world's shipping, over half of this total being British. That the submarine did not win the war at sea for the Germans was due firstly to the convoy system and secondly to the entry of America into the war, whereby the building rate of merchant ships exceeded the sinkings.

Before the war was over Britain built the 'M' class of which one boat was completed. *M.1* (Plate VII) carried one 12-inch gun, the principle being that, since the torpedo armament of the standard submarine of the day could not sink a Dreadnought, a vessel which could bring a very big gun to bear at 1000 yards range might be more effective. *M.1* was never tried in war but, as a type, was a success.

By now the reliability of the submarine was something which the navies of the world accepted. Perhaps the best example of this was the British 'H' class. First laid down in 1915 these small handy boats of 500 tons with four 21-inch bow torpedo tubes went about their business with great confidence. Those built in the United States for Britain happily crossed the Atlantic without assistance.

When peace came Great Britain was left the undisputed major sea power and somewhat strangely began building ingenious experimental submarines, thus developing the very weapon which had so nearly brought her to defeat. The most successful British submarine in the war had been the 'E' class, carrying two 18-inch tubes in the bow, one single on each beam and one single astern. It was decided that heavier torpedo armament was preferable to the 12-inch gun of the 'M' class and the submarine must be able to sink a major war vessel. This policy resulted in the L.50 class, carrying six torpedo tubes in the bow and an increase in size of the torpedo itself from 18 inches to 21 inches.

At the same time anti-submarine measures were not overlooked and twelve boats of the 'R' class (Plate VI) were built with high underwater speed and a salvo of six 18-inch torpedoes, solely to sink another submarine. Also, determined to keep the lead in construction, the hull of one of the abandoned 'M' class was used to build the first submarine aircraft carrier, M.2 (Plate VIII). This boat was fitted with a hangar and provided with a reconnaissance Parnell Peto seaplane which could be launched from the surface by catapult. The aeroplane had an endurance of two hours flying time at the end of which it had to be either at its home base or back on board its parent submarine.*

In 1925 yet another experimental submarine was built. This was X.1, of 3000 tons, carrying four 5.2-inch guns and a salvo of six 21-inch torpedoes. This ship was superior to the destroyer of the day and was really a commerce raider, the last type which Britain wanted to emphasize. X.1 had trouble with her engines and so was scrapped. It is odd that the Board of Admiralty should ever have ordered the building of such a ship. Belated propaganda decrying the value of this submarine did not deter the French from building the Surcouf (Plate IX) in 1927, fitted with two 8-inch guns and carrying a spotter seaplane, her avowed prime purpose being commerce raiding.

The final British experiment was M.3, a minelayer with increased capacity from the 18 mines carried internally in a standard submarine to 100 all carried externally.

Germany's part in the evolution of the submarine from the end of the First World War was governed at first by the 1918 Treaty of Versailles, which allowed no submarines to be kept by the Germans and forbade the construction or acquisition of any submarine even for commercial purposes. However, in the late nineteen-twenties she began building in Holland, training her crews abroad also.

Meanwhile Britain had returned to the St Vincent policy and at the Washington Naval Conference of 1921 strongly advocated abolition, but this was opposed, mainly by France and the United States. While limitations of surface naval armaments were achieved in the Washington Treaty, no limit was put on the number of submarines. The next move was made in the London Naval Treaty of 1931. The principal naval powers held this conference because the Washington Treaty of 1921 was due to expire in 1936. Again Great Britain advocated abolition, this time supported by Italy, and some limitation in submarines was arrived at. However, a major change came about in 1935 when Hitler repudiated the Versailles Treaty. Great Britain immediately concluded the Anglo-German Naval Agreement and special provision was made for Germany to build up to 100 per cent of British tonnage at some future date, should the situation warrant it. In 1938 Hitler invoked this clause, although there was no justification for it and against all the protests from Britain and other maritime nations.

Finally, after Munich, the German 'Z plan' was put into force which authorised the building of 300 submarines by 1945 for the express purpose of defeating Great Britain. The submarine was again playing a most important part in international affairs.

By the end of the nineteen-twenties British submarine experiments had died down and development in building in the navies of the world, uncontrolled by restrictive clauses in treaties, had settled down to a standard form. The British concentrated on boats of 500 and 1000 tons. The United States with the Pacific Ocean to cover built a large 3000-ton

type, the 'V' class, carrying two 6-inch guns. The Japanese, being the weaker naval power in that area, built up a formidable submarine fleet with some boats of 2000 tons. The French too went in for quantity and built more submarines than either Britain or the United States.

The Second World War found the British supremely confident in the capability of the Asdic underwater detection device for tracking submarines submerged which it was believed would drive the enemy submarines from the oceans. This did not happen as the Germans operated on the surface using 'wolf packs' to attack convoys at night. First they concentrated their force, then moved into the centre of the convoy under cover of darkness and fired their torpedoes, also from the surface. These tactics were immediately successful and once again the submarine came near to winning the war at sea. That it did not do so this time was due to the Germans sacrificing their main objectives for subsidiaries, such as augmenting the Italians in the Mediterranean and covering the Norwegian coast against the possibility of an allied invasion. To these faulty appreciations, which deprived the Atlantic force of the means of reaching a decisive position, was added considerable allied scientific advancements, the principal of which was radar.

Through this invention the German 'wolf packs' were driven from the surface and forced to dive. There was a time when there were no enemy submarines in the Atlantic at all. For the Germans to continue their attack on commerce with any effect it was now necessary to increase underwater speed so that their submarines when submerged could still close on the convoys and then surface and complete the attack under cover of darkness. By delaying surfacing until very close to the convoy the effect of radar was virtually nullified, and the Asdic, at best, had only a couple of miles or so in which to warn the Commodore of the convoy.

Meanwhile, through the schnorkel tube, an invention which the Germans were the first to put to practical use and whereby the submarine could take in air to its diesel engines when submerged, greater underwater endurance was obtained. The top of the schnorkel tube was difficult to spot on radar and when in use the boats were still in comparative safety.

Coupled with this improvement, which greatly conserved battery power, the Germans doubled the electric power for submerged propulsion, necessitating larger electric batteries which in turn dictated the size of the submarines. In some cases this too was doubled, but this was not a disadvantage because these longer boats were better for streamlining.

The Germans named these types 'XXI' and 'XXIII'. Both classes could do 18 knots submerged, a speed well sufficient to intercept convoys. Later the German Professor Walther produced an engine for submerged propulsion which ran on a high concentration of hydrogen peroxide – 'ingolin'. This engine, by reason of needing no air, brought the development of the true submarine vessel a stage nearer, but the war ended before a force fitted with these engines, type 'XXVI', could be got to sea.

Whereas the schnorkel allowed German submarines to patrol for three weeks off the Cape of Good Hope, the Walther boats, type 'XXVI', would have had a greater impact on operations and if they had been disposed to the best advantage to attack commerce they might well have become decisive.

Typical German submarines of the Second World War were the 'VIIB' class, of which U.99 was one (Plate X). This submarine was commanded by Otto Kretschmer, now Admiral Commanding the German Naval Forces.

In the Pacific the Americans made the most of the submarine's offensive power by using it against the enemy fleet, as well as the merchant fleet. In their war against Japan, United States submarines sank one third of the Japanese Navy, the greatest tonnage of warships ever sunk by submarines, thus elevating the submarine to the position of the

---

* Both M.1 and M.2 were lost on diving patrols. The former was hit by a merchant ship and the latter sank because the hangar door was opened too soon when surfacing to fly off the aircraft.

principal warship of a major sea power. Typical of the submarines which achieved this success was the *Balao* (Plate XI).

The Japanese were not so successful, either against warships or commerce. They had difficulty in finding their targets and built eleven submarines each carrying a small reconnaissance seaplane in an endeavour to improve this position. Towards the end of the war the Japanese built five large aircraft carriers (Plate XIII) offensively armed with three bombers. This force actually set out to bomb the Panama Canal, only to be halted by the war coming to an end.

During the war Great Britain, Italy, Japan and Germany all built midget submarines of various designs, or derivatives of this type of weapon such as human torpedoes. It was like going back to the days of Bushnell. The first attack was made in 1940 by the Italians on ships in the entrance to the Admiralty harbour at Gibraltar which was unsuccessful. The most famous attack was made by British 'X' craft (Plate XII), in 1943, on the German Battleship Tirpitz lying in Kåfjord in northern Norway. Two of these midget submarines were successful and the battleship was badly damaged. Earlier, in 1941, Italian human torpedoes had attacked and damaged the British battleships *Queen Elizabeth* and *Valiant* in Alexandria harbour. The Japanese took five midget submarines to Pearl Harbour but they were unsuccessful. Towards the end of the war British midgets in the Far East cut cables and attacked Japanese warships with success. The Germans also tried midgets; their '*Seehunds*' were used during the allied invasion of Europe but, although well designed, never succeeded operationally. All these attacks were worthwhile but the midgets were specialised craft and did not advance the evolution of the submarine proper.

Once again summarising the evolution of the submarine at the end of a world war, it can be said that it had proved itself equal to, if not superior to, any surface warship in the major task of sinking the enemy's heavy ships.

In operations against commerce its power was temporarily restricted by radar, but with the introduction of type 'XXVI' this could have been largely overcome and again the submarine might have been decisive.

Thus in both spheres of naval warfare, the sinking of enemy naval ships and enemy commerce, in the hands of the Americans and the Germans respectively in the Second World War the submarine had become the supreme warship.

CHAPTER VII

The Nuclear Age

On 17th January 1955 the U.S.S. *Nautilus* left the Electric Boat Company's pier at Groton, Connecticut, and silently moved out into the Thames river. As she swung into the main channel she flashed the dramatic signal, 'Under way on nuclear power.'

Since the end of the Second World War the victorious powers had experimented with the various types of captured German submarines allotted to them following the division and dispersion of the German fleet. The Russians introduced a full-scale building programme, outstripping all other countries in numbers of conventionally-powered, schnorkel-equipped, ocean-going submarines, and by 1960 had a fleet of 450 boats. In contrast, the United States went steadily along the course of improved propulsion systems. She was well equipped to do this with her undamaged shipyards, her research facilities and her money. Great Britain did much the same but on a smaller scale and, as not uncommonly, achieved the earlier greater success, particularly with the Walther power plant, and in two unarmed boats, *Explorer* and *Excalibur*, achieved underwater speeds of 25 knots.

Meanwhile, behind all this varied effort there was always the certainty that one day nuclear power could be applied to the submarine, thus bringing into being at long last the true submarine which could virtually remain submerged for ever, and completing its evolution. One man who brought this dream to practical life was Rear Admiral Hyman Rickover, U.S.N., an engineer and a submariner. In 1946 Rickover was a Captain. He had before him much preliminary work by Dr Ross Gunn of the Naval Research Laboratory and Dr Philip H. Abelson of the Carnegie Institute.

The project of a nuclear reactor took root at Park Ridge, Tennessee, and for nine years Rickover overcame doubt, hostility, apathy, lack of funds, lack of materials, and much else besides. During this time he was passed over for promotion, and only at the last moment, when the submarine reactor was on the verge of completion, did the authorities begin to realise what this man had done for the United States, and, indeed, for the world. The name of Rickover will go down in the history of the submarine with those of Fulton, Laubeuf and Holland.

Nautilus (Plate XIV) was 320 feet long and of 3539 tons surface displacement. She carried six bow torpedo tubes with three reloads. She was a complete success. In May 1955 she sailed submerged from New London, Connecticut, to San Juan, Puerto Rico, a distance of 1381 miles, at an average submerged speed of 16 knots. In comparison with any other boat this was ninety times longer than any submarine had ever steamed at such high speed submerged. In short, all submarine records were broken. But most of all, here was the true submarine which need never surface, possessing a power plant which could run without air and required fuel only once every couple of years. All this might have been brought to naught but for the parallel advance in air purifying, nicknamed by the Americans 'the CO_2 Scrubber', and equally important advances in the generation of oxygen.

Nautilus was also fitted with diesel engines for use in case anything went wrong with the nuclear reactor. Because of the diesel she had a schnorkel by which the air in the boat could be completely changed in twenty minutes if operational conditions allowed.

Since she had no need to fill much of the boat with oil fuel tanks and batteries, there was room for every improvement in living conditions for her crew of ten officers and ninety-three men. There were bunks for everyone, air conditioning to keep the interior between 68 and 72 degrees Fahrenheit, and the humidity at an even 50 per cent. There were clothes-washing machines, laboratories, and a library with 600 books.

After two years *Nautilus* had steamed more than 62,500 miles, 36,500 of which had been submerged. The time had come to make history once again, and under the command of Commander William R. Anderson in August 1958 the submarine passed over the North Pole under ice. Without altering course, one moment she was steaming due north, and the next her head was due south. Before this remarkable voyage had taken place the project had received the attention of innumerable senior officers, senators, scientists and the President himself. This was not merely because of the novelty of the idea, but by making this passage and thus linking the Atlantic and Pacific Oceans all the year round, strategic thinking in the navies of the world had been changed.

From these beginnings the first production model nuclear attack submarines were built: *Skate*, *Swordfish*, *Sargo* and *Seadragon* were all commissioned before the end of 1959. All four had similar power plants which, through technical advances, had been made smaller than the original in *Nautilus*. Moreover, the boats themselves were smaller—268 feet instead of 321, and 2550 tons instead of 3539. *Skate*, the first off the production line, lost no time in establishing her name in history as she succeeded in surfacing through the ice at the North Pole.

Thoughts now turned to adapting the nuclear submarine to the needs of the Navy as a whole. It was recalled that in the spring of 1944, around Okinawa, 34 radar picket ships and supporting gunboats were sunk. Some 300 more were damaged, with the total loss of 4000 men killed and 5000 wounded. Submersible radar picket ships could have saved this loss of life. The result was the U.S.S. *Triton*, launched in August 1958 and commissioned a little more than a year later. *Triton* was the largest and most powerful submarine of her day. She was powered by two nuclear reactors, and is still the only submarine with two. The size of a light cruiser, 5700 tons on the surface and 8000 submerged, and with a length of $447\frac{1}{2}$ feet, she was a monster. With 15 officers and 159 men in her crew, of whom 33 were Chief Petty Officers, she carried more talent than any previous submarine. Obviously something special and spectacular had to come from this magnificent boat. High level conferences were called, and at the conclusion Captain Beach, the Commanding Officer, was ordered to circumnavigate the globe submerged. Between 16th February and 25th April 1960 *Triton* went round the world, including an additional 2000 miles to transfer a sick rating to a surface ship, which was done without bringing the pressure hull above water, so keeping to the letter of the order. The time-table of this historic underwater voyage is worthy of record:

February 16   Submerged off Long Island.
         24   Off St Paul Rocks. Cross the equator.

March   5   Partially surfaced off Montevideo to disembark sick rating.
         7   Rounded Cape Horn.
      13   Passed Easter Island.
      25   Passed Hawaiian Islands.
      28   Passed Guam.

April   1   Passed Philippine Islands.
         5   Passed through Lombok Strait, Indonesia.
      17   Round Cape of Good Hope.
      25   Passed St Paul Rocks and completed submerged navigation of globe.

Meanwhile throughout the 1950s some quiet thinking had been going on. Minds went back to the 'Hollands' and their interesting shape. The primary objective of this decade of study was speed under water. For the public it was announced that nuclear submarines were capable of speeds of over 20 knots. This statement stands today and rightly, because it would not be in the interest of the Western World to say more, but it can be assumed that the most modern nuclear submarines are capable of speeds well over the official 20 knots. The British publication *Jane's Fighting Ships* gives U.S.S. *Skipjack* a speed of 35 knots submerged.

It was the shape of the 'Holland' boats which inspired the designers to build the *Albacore* entirely for hydrodynamic research. Hitherto, except for the British 'R' class, all sub-

marines were in fact submersibles designed principally with surface ship capabilities, especially in the ratio between length and breadth. *Albacore* was designed purely for underwater work with a length/breadth ratio of 3:1 instead of the 5 or 6:1 of the submersibles. In addition *Albacore* was given a very small superstructure and was powered only by electric batteries. She did her job well and her performance led the designers to build the U.S.S. *Skipjack* (Plate XV). They gave this boat a blunt nose, shaped her like a rugby football and stripped her of the normal casing and upper deck fittings while retaining the large fin superstructure and forward hydroplanes. She was a true submarine in basic shape and marked a clear step forward in evolution. *Skipjack* varied further from her predecessors in that she was given only one propeller which was slow-moving, the intention being to cut down noise.

When *Skipjack* did her trials in August 1959 she went deeper for longer than any previous submarine. The scene was now set to build an underwater navy. There was much forward thinking to do. The Soviets had put a man into space, and their rocketry had developed to fantastic proportions. Their submarine fleet, hitherto an enlargement of Second World War types, would shortly be turning to nuclear power. The Americans determined on two immediate projects.

Following successful trials in the 1950s with 'Regulus' missiles in conventional submarines they built the *Halibut*, the first nuclear submarine to have missile armament. *Halibut* was the same size as *Triton* and had to surface to fire her missiles. It was intended that she would operate in the Pacific. Secondly, 'killer' submarines were needed to hunt and destroy enemy nuclear submarines, and for this purpose they built the *Tullibee*, the smallest of the nuclear submarines in displacement. Even so, she was of 2318 tons on the surface. She was packed with sonar equipment. Both these ships were commissioned in 1960.

Up to this time the Americans had behaved in the 1950s and early 1960s rather as the French did at the end of the nineteenth century and the British after the First World War, by building numerous different submarines. The time had come to standardise, as the Germans did in the First World War. Accordingly, *Thresher* was designed from the best of *Skipjack* and *Tullibee*.

Thresher was lost in a disaster in 1963, so the *Permit*, the next ship in sequence, became the named ship of the class, of which 22 were laid down at once, and these added to by as many as 34 'Sturgeon' class, an improved version of the 'Permit' class. All these submarines are supplied with propelled missiles and homing torpedoes, launched from their 4 torpedo tubes. Experiments and exercises with the first of these two classes have changed all the old concepts of naval warfare. Indeed, the war at sea in the future will be fought primarily under water in three dimensions.

All these spectacular advances in the evolution of the submarine, it might be supposed, would have placed the Western World under a sure shield of United States sea power, but sea power had to take note of the advent of nuclear weapons. The disturbing Russian advance in the strategic missile field, widened by their putting the first 'sputnik' into orbit and their programme of atmospheric tests of nuclear weapons, set the United States on a further programme. The basic policy had been considered in the days of the building of the *Nautilus* and kept in cold storage. Now, in the late 1950s, it was quickly unfrozen. Hitherto the nuclear submarine programme had been one of 'attack', but now the submarines were to be used as the greatest weapon for defence and to be developed into what has been called 'the ultimate deterrent'.

It was as far back as 1955 that a junior admiral, William F. Raborn, was selected to develop a dependable strategic ballistic missile and the submarine to launch it 'within the next ten years'. With the danger signs already developing before his eyes, Admiral Raborn decided that ten years was too long. Soon this thinking was reflected in the minds of the Chief of Naval Operations and the Secretary of the Navy.

Raborn's project was made top priority. Like Rickover he was a man who knew how to get a job done, and in his task he was equally successful. On 20th July 1960, years ahead of schedule, an American submarine fired two Polaris missiles while entirely submerged. The missiles hurtled 1100 miles down the Atlantic missile range with perfect accuracy. On 15th December of the same year, the U.S. Submarine *George Washington* (Plate XVI) sailed from Charleston, South Carolina, to patrol for two months somewhere in the North Atlantic. This great ship, of 5960 tons surface displacement and armed with 16 Polaris missiles, was the most powerful warship the world had ever known and in her primary role of deploying the deterrent is virtually immune from anti-submarine measures. She has been followed by no less than 40 others of similar, but latterly improved, capability which, when deployed, will present a deterrent force of unmatched magnitude.

In all this, Great Britain, for so long the greatest sea power, has followed suit and now possesses seven nuclear submarines, four of which will be Polaris-armed, and has others under construction. The French, too, do not intend their part in the evolution of the submarine to fade entirely and are moving in the same direction.

Thus the submarine has now come full circle. From Bourne and Van Drebbel's peaceful experiment to its development as a warship in the nineteenth century, mostly by the versatile French, it became in the early 1900s the weapon of the weaker Power, and later, through two world wars, it was found to be a 'war winner' in the hands of major Powers. Now, in the second half of the twentieth century, the submarine carries perhaps the greatest responsibility of all time, for on its presence in the oceans the peace of the world chiefly depends.

Notes

1. S B = Submersible. A vessel operating on the two propulsion system.
   S M = A true submarine. A vessel operating on one propulsion system and having no need to surface.
   British R (No. 8) has been classified as both S B and S M as it was the nearest approach to the true submarine before the advent of nuclear power.
2. All S Bs (i.e. Nos. 1–13 inclusive) relied on electric battery power for submerged propulsion.
3. The statistics in the table are given as a background to the text and the information is relevant to the development of the story. The table does not represent all known facts and figures of the submarines selected.

NATIONALITY	DATE	TYPE	LENGTH BEAM DRAUGHT	DISPLACEMENT (tons)		ENGINES
				SURFACE	SUBMERGED	
1. FRENCH	1898 1899	Narval S B	111' 6" 12' 4" 5' 3"	106	168	Steam triple expansion one screw
2. BRITISH	1901 1902	Holland S B	63' 6" 11' 10" 5' 6"	105	120	Petrol one screw
3. GERMAN	1914	U 35 S B	212' 20'	685	844	Diesel twin screws
4. GERMAN	1916	Merchant ship U 151 S B	213' 29' 15'	1512	1875	Diesel twin screws
5. BRITISH	1917	K 26 S B	351' 28' 16' 10"	1750	2450	Parsons and Brown Curtis steam turbines two screws
6. BRITISH	1918	R S B S M	163' 15' 9" 10'	410	500	Diesel one screw
7. BRITISH	1918	M 1 S B	305' 28' 15' 9"	1650	1950	Diesel twin screws
8. BRITISH	1920	M 2 S B	305' 28' 15' 9"	1650	1950	Diesel twin screws
9. FRENCH	1929	Surcouf S B	360' 29' 6" 23'	3304	4218	Diesel twin screws
10. GERMAN	1940	U 99 S B	218' 20' 15'		857	Diesel electric twin screws
11. AMERICAN	1942	Balao S B	307' 27' 17' 6"	1800	2455	4 diesel electric on two shafts
12. BRITISH	1943	X Craft Midget	51' 8' 6" 10'	35		Diesel
13. JAPANESE	1944	I 400 S B	380' 39' 23'	5223	6560	4 sets diesel on two shafts
14. AMERICAN	1954	Nautilus S M	338' 29' 22'	3765	4260	Nuclear twin screws
15. AMERICAN	1958	Skipjack S M	252' 32' 28'	3075	3500	Nuclear one screw
16. AMERICAN	1959	George Washington S M	382' 33' 29'	6010	6700	Nuclear one screw

See notes on page 35

TORPEDO TUBES	GUNS	OTHER	COMPLEMENT		PERFORMANCE (knots)		REMARKS
			OFFICERS	RATINGS	SURFACE	SUBMERGED	
2 17.75″ each side upper deck	–	–	14		9.8	5.3	Torpedoes fired from 2 Drzewiecki upper deck frames each side
1 18″	–	–	2	7	8.5	7	Originally designed without a periscope
4 19.7″ 2 bow 2 stern	1 or 2 3.4″ or 1 4.1″	–	32–39		16.4	9.7	Typical first World War
*2 19.7″	2 5.9″ or 2 4.1″	–	56		12.4	5.2	*Merchant ship Deutschland made 2 voyages to USA in 1916. Converted to U cruiser
6 18″ bow 4 18″ beam	2 4″ 1 3″ AA	–	5	45	23.5	10	Designed to operate with Fleet.
6 18″ bow	–	–	2	20	9½	15	First anti submarine submarine
4 18″ bow	1 12″ Mark IX 1 3″ AA		6	59	14	8	The only big gun submarine
4 18″ bow	1 3″ AA	1 Parnell Peto Seaplane	6	59 2 air crew	14 3840 @ 10	8	First submersible aircraft carrier
6 550 mm internal (4 bow, 2 stern) 4 400 mm external in revolving mountings	2 8″, 2 37 mm cannon AA, 48 mm AA.	1 Besson MB 411 two-seater seaplane.	8	110	18	8½	Cruiser type commerce destroyer. Seaplane had a range of 215 miles at 81 mph
4 21″ bow 1 21″ stern	1 3.5″ 1 20 mm AA		44		17½	10	Schnorkel tube added later. Also 3.5″ gun removed 1 37 mm and 1 extra 20 mm AA added.
6 21″ bow 21″ stern	1 4.5″ 2 40 mm AA		8	75	18	9	Typical of US submersibles World War II with both submerged and surface capabilities. 12 000 mile radius of action, Fitted with radar.
2 Saddle charges 2 tons of amatex			3 1 qualified diver	1	6½	5	Surface endurance 1500 @ 4. Submerged 80 @ 2.
8 21″ bow	1 5.5″ 10 25 mm AA	3 Bombers (total armament 4 torpedoes, 3 800 kg & 12 250 kg bombs).	144		30 000 m @ 16 K^n 37 000 m @ 14 K^n		The largest *submersible* ever built and the largest submersible aircraft carrier.
6 21″ bow			10	95	20	23	Nuclear powered prototype
6 21″ bow			8	85	20	35	Hunter Killer
6 21″ bow	16 missile launching tubes		12	100	20	28	Polaris. The 'Ultimate Deterrent'.

The colour plates

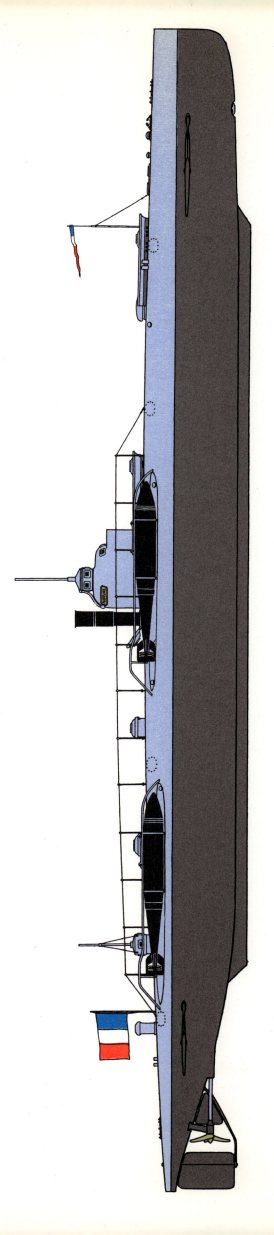

French

Narval 1898–9

LENGTH O/A: 111 ft 6 in

BEAM: 12 ft 4 in

DRAUGHT: 5 ft 3 in

DISPLACEMENT
Surface: 106 tons
Submerged: 168 tons

ARMAMENT
Torpedo tubes: Four 17.75-in

PROPULSION
Surface: Steam
Submerged: Electric

SPEED
Surface: 9.8 knots
Submerged: 5.3 knots

COMPLEMENT: 14

Holland Class 1901–2

British

LENGTH O/A: 63 ft 6 in

BEAM: 11 ft 10 in

DRAUGHT: 5 ft 6 in

DISPLACEMENT
Surface: 105 tons
Submerged: 120 tons

ARMAMENT
Torpedo tubes: One 18-in

PROPULSION
Surface: Petrol
Submerged: Electric

SPEED
Surface: 8.5 knots
Submerged: 7 knots

COMPLEMENT
Officers: 2
Ratings: 7

U 35 1914

German

LENGTH O/A: 212 ft

BEAM: 20 ft

DRAUGHT: 12 ft

DISPLACEMENT
Surface: 685 tons
Submerged: 844 tons

PROPULSION
Surface: Diesel
Submerged: Electric

SPEED
Surface: 16.4 knots
Submerged: 9.7 knots

COMPLEMENT: 32–39

ARMAMENT
Torpedo tubes: Four 19.7-in
Guns: One or two 3.4-in or one 4.1-in

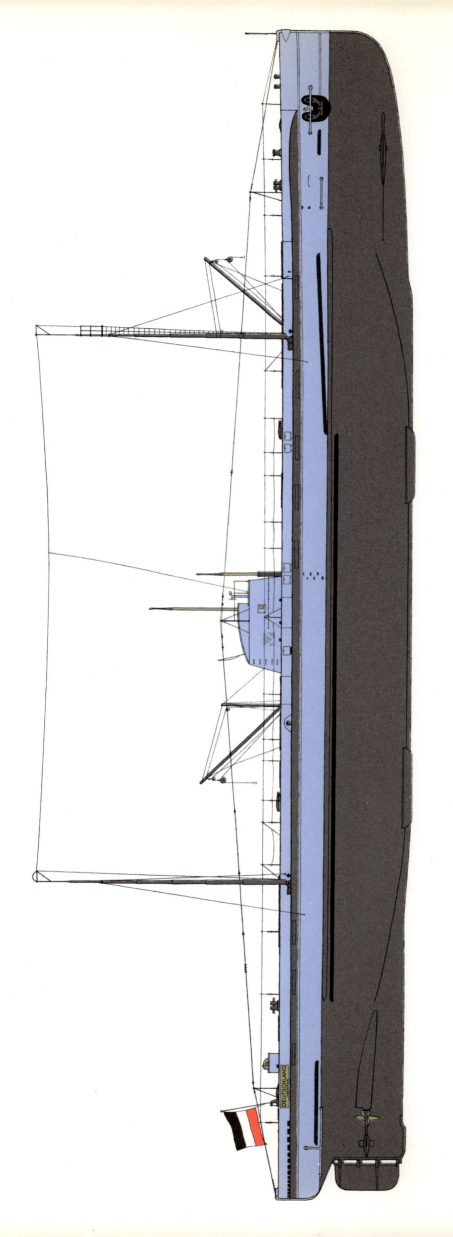

Deutschland 1916

German

PROPULSION
Surface: Diesel
Submerged: Electric

SPEED
Surface: 12.4 knots
Submerged: 5.2 knots

COMPLEMENT: 56

LENGTH O/A: 213 ft

BEAM: 29 ft
DRAUGHT: 15 ft

DISPLACEMENT
Surface: 1512 tons
Submerged: 1875 tons

ARMAMENT (on conversion)
Torpedo tubes: Two 19.7-in
Guns: Two 5.9-in or two 4.1-in

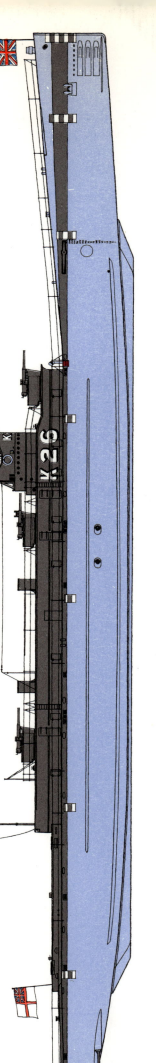

K 26 1917

British

LENGTH O/A: 351 ft

BEAM: 28 ft

DRAUGHT: 16 ft 10 in

DISPLACEMENT
Surface: 1750 tons
Submerged: 2450 tons

ARMAMENT
Torpedo tubes: Ten 18-in
Guns: Two 4-in, one 3-in AA

PROPULSION
Surface: Steam
Submerged: Electric

SPEED
Surface: 23.5 knots
Submerged: 10 knots

COMPLEMENT
Officers: 5
Ratings: 45

R Class 1918

LENGTH O/A: 163 ft

BEAM: 15 ft 9 in

DRAUGHT: 10 ft

DISPLACEMENT
Surface: 410 tons
Submerged: 500 tons

ARMAMENT
Torpedo tubes: Six 18-in

PROPULSION
Surface: Diesel
Submerged: Electric

SPEED
Surface: 9.5 knots
Submerged: 15 knots

COMPLEMENT
Officers: 2
Ratings: 20

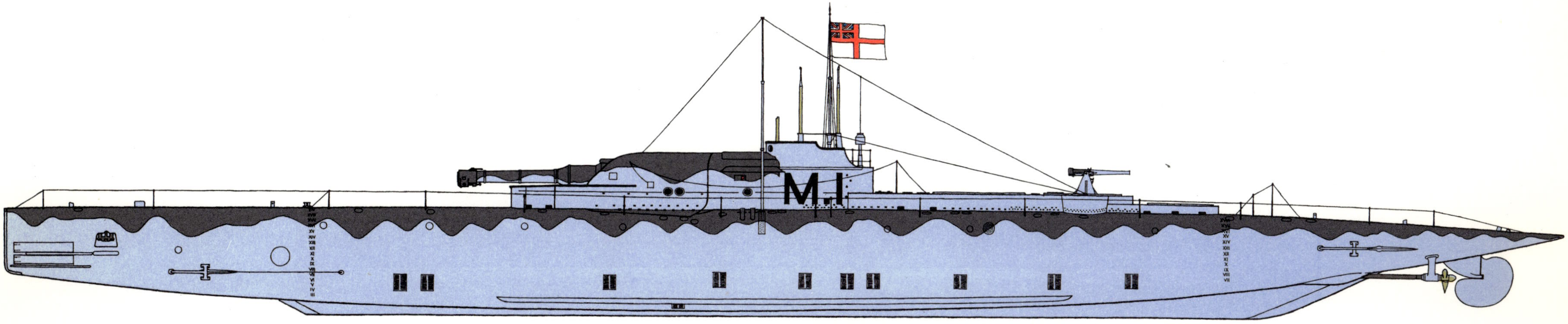

M1 1918

British

LENGTH O/A: 305 ft

BEAM: 28 ft

DRAUGHT: 15 ft 9 in

DISPLACEMENT
Surface: 1650 tons
Submerged: 1950 tons

ARMAMENT
Torpedo tubes: Four 18-in
Guns: One 12-in, one 3-in AA

PROPULSION
Surface: Diesel
Submerged: Electric

SPEED
Surface: 14 knots
Submerged: 8 knots

COMPLEMENT
Officers: 6
Ratings: 59

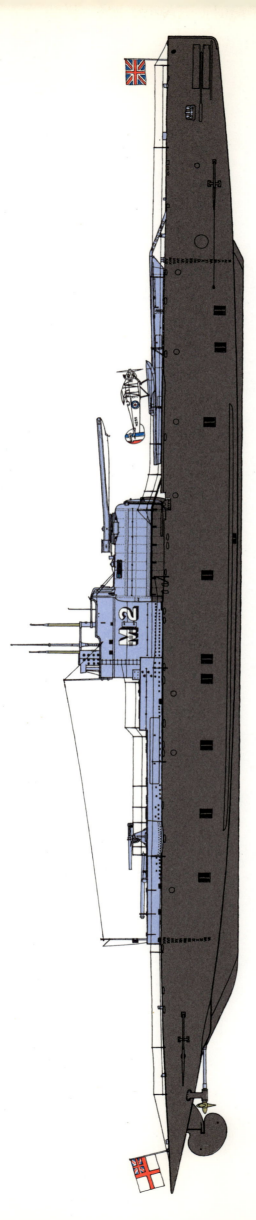

M 2 1920

LENGTH O/A: 305 ft

BEAM: 28 ft

DRAUGHT: 15 ft 9 in

DISPLACEMENT
Surface: 1650 tons
Submerged: 1950 tons

ARMAMENT
Torpedo tubes: Four 18-in
Guns: One 3-in AA
Other: One seaplane

PROPULSION
Surface: Diesel
Submerged: Electric

SPEED
Surface: 14 knots
Submerged: 8 knots

COMPLEMENT
Officers: 6
Ratings: 59
Other: 2 Air crew

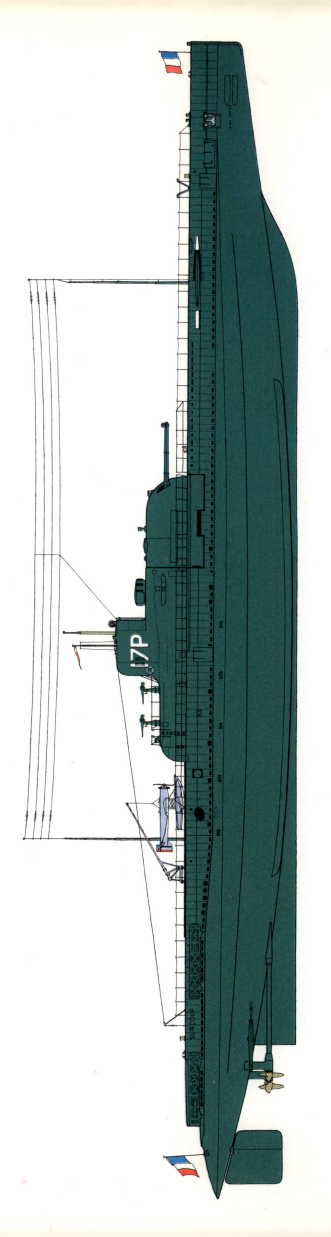

Surcouf 1929

French

LENGTH O/A: 360 ft

BEAM: 29 ft 6 in

DRAUGHT: 23 ft

DISPLACEMENT
Surface: 3304 tons
Submerged: 4218 tons

ARMAMENT
Torpedo tubes: Ten 550/400-mm
Guns: Two 8-in, two 37-mm AA, four 8-mm AA

Other: One seaplane

PROPULSION
Surface: Diesel
Submerged: Electric

SPEED
Surface: 18 knots
Submerged: 8.5 knots

COMPLEMENT
Officers: 8
Ratings: 110

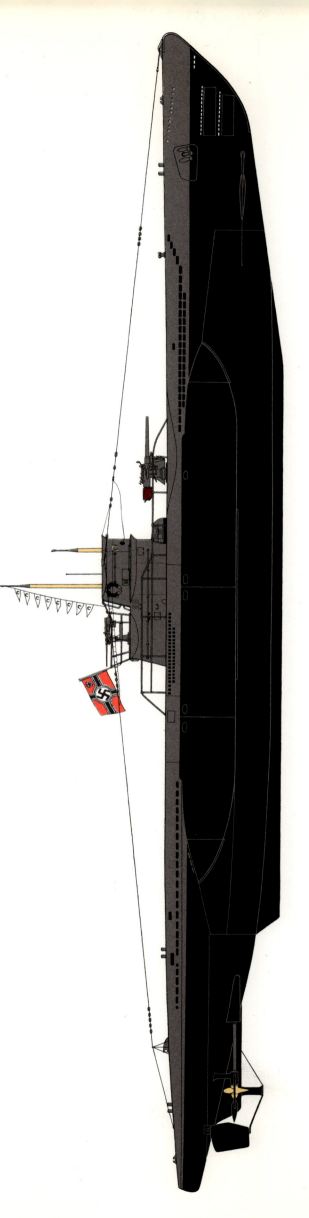

U 99 1940

German

LENGTH O/A: 218 ft

BEAM: 20 ft

DRAUGHT: 15 ft

DISPLACEMENT
Surface: 753 tons
Submerged: 857 tons

ARMAMENT
Torpedo tubes: Five 21-in
Guns: One 3.5-in, one 20-mm AA

PROPULSION
Surface: Diesel electric
Submerged: Electric

SPEED
Surface: 17.5 knots
Submerged: 10 knots

COMPLEMENT: 44

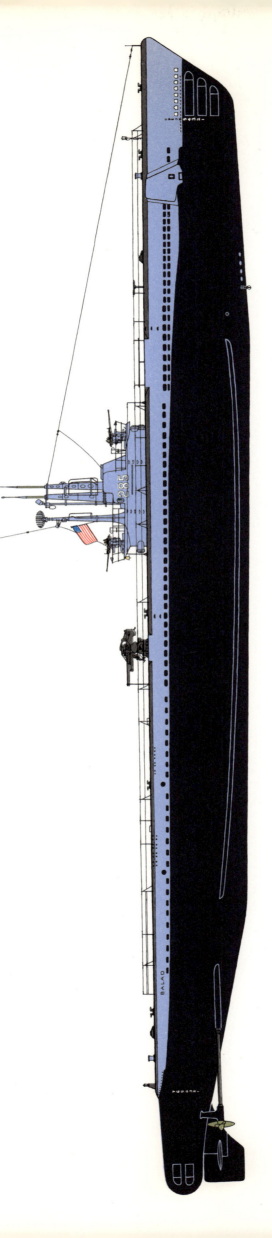

American

Balao 1942

LENGTH O/A: 307 ft

BEAM: 27 ft

DRAUGHT: 17 ft 6 in

DISPLACEMENT
Surface: 1800 tons
Submerged: 2455 tons

ARMAMENT
Torpedo tubes: Ten 21-in
Guns: One 4.5-in, two 40-mm AA

PROPULSION
Surface: Diesel electric
Submerged: Electric

SPEED
Surface: 18 knots
Submerged: 9 knots

COMPLEMENT
Officers: 8
Ratings: 75

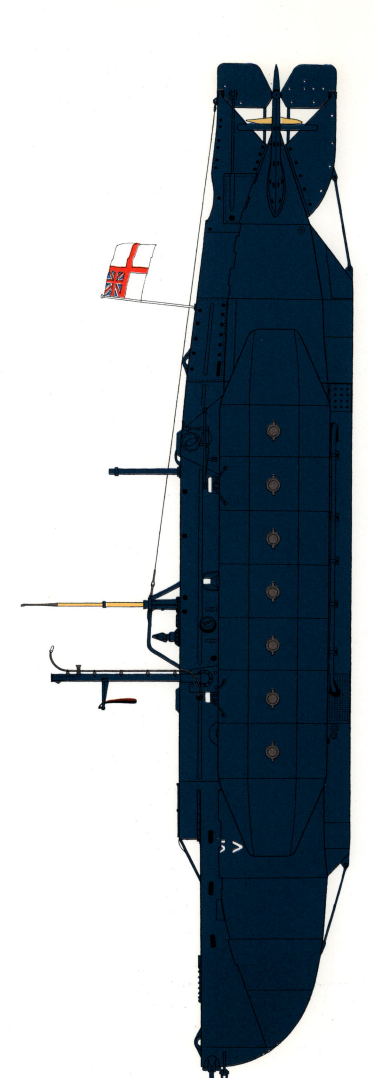

British

X Craft 1943

LENGTH O/A: 51 ft

BEAM: 8 ft 6 in

DRAUGHT: 10 ft

DISPLACEMENT
Surface: 35 tons

ARMAMENT
Two saddle charges, two tons of amatex

PROPULSION
Surface: Diesel
Submerged: Electric

SPEED
Surface: 6.5 knots
Submerged: 5 knots

COMPLEMENT
Officers: 3
Ratings: 2

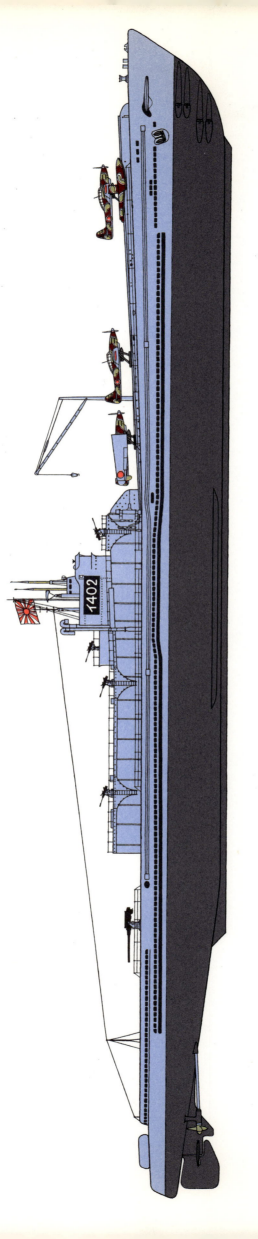

I 400 1944

Japanese

LENGTH O/A: 380 ft

BEAM: 39 ft

DRAUGHT: 23 ft

DISPLACEMENT
Surface: 5223 tons
Submerged: 6560 tons

ARMAMENT
Torpedo tubes: Eight 21-in

Guns: One 5.5-in, ten 25-mm AA
Other: Three bombers

PROPULSION
Surface: Diesel
Submerged: Electric

PERFORMANCE
30,000 miles at 16 knots
37,000 miles at 14 knots

COMPLEMENT: 144

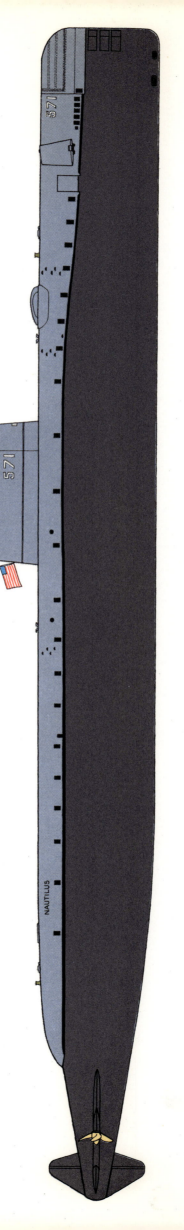

American

Nautilus 1954

LENGTH O/A: 338 ft

BEAM: 29 ft

DRAUGHT: 22 ft

DISPLACEMENT
Surface: 3765 tons
Submerged: 4260 tons

ARMAMENT
Torpedo tubes: Six 21-in

PROPULSION: Nuclear

SPEED
Surface: 20 knots
Submerged: 23 knots

COMPLEMENT
Officers: 10
Ratings: 95

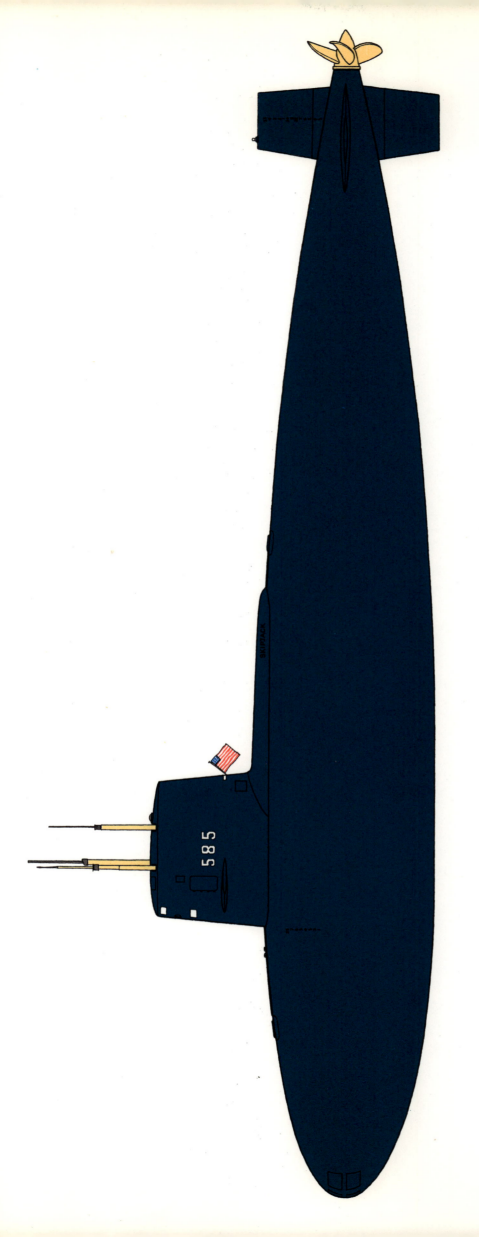

Skipjack 1958

American

LENGTH O/A: 252 ft

BEAM: 32 ft

DRAUGHT: 28 ft

DISPLACEMENT
Surface: 3075 tons
Submerged: 3500 tons

ARMAMENT
Torpedo tubes: Six 21-in

PROPULSION: Nuclear

SPEED
Surface: 20 knots
Submerged: 35 knots

COMPLEMENT
Officers: 8
Ratings: 85

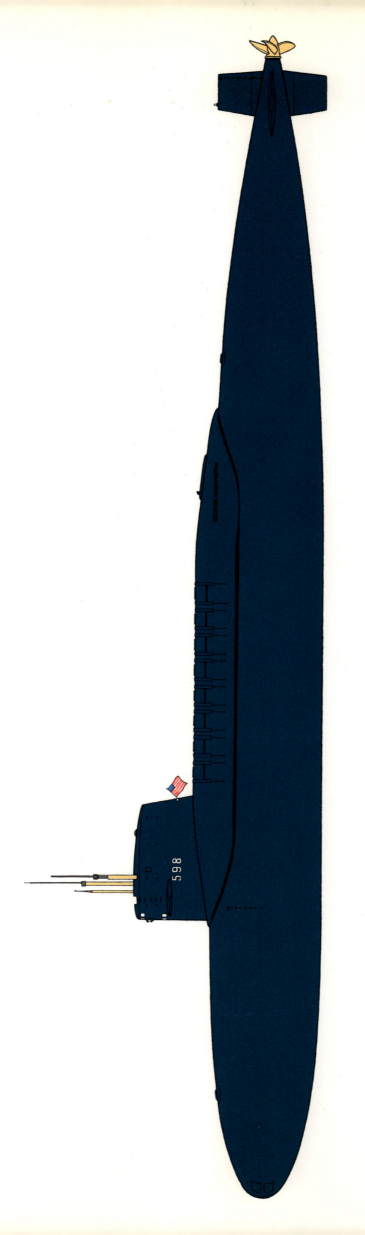

George Washington 1959 *American*

LENGTH O/A: 382 ft

BEAM: 33 ft

DRAUGHT: 29 ft

DISPLACEMENT
Surface: 6010 tons
Submerged: 6700 tons

ARMAMENT
Torpedo tubes: Six 21-in
Other: Sixteen missile launching tubes

PROPULSION: Nuclear

SPEED
Surface: 20 knots
Submerged: 28 knots

COMPLEMENT
Officers: 12
Ratings: 100